JavaScript Mastery

From Beginner to Full-Stack Developer Learn JavaScript fundamentals, frontend frameworks, and backend development

THOMPSON CARTER

Table of Content

TABLE OF CONTENTS

Introduction

Building Modern Web Applications with JavaScript: From Frontend to Backend"

In today's world of technology, web development has become an integral part of nearly every business, service, and application. As businesses increasingly rely on digital solutions, the demand for capable web developers continues to rise. JavaScript, once a simple client-side scripting language, has evolved into one of the most powerful and versatile tools in the world of web development. From creating dynamic user interfaces to handling backend logic and server-side development, JavaScript has solidified its place as the backbone of modern web applications.

This book, *Building Modern Web Applications with JavaScript: From Frontend to Backend*, is designed to guide both beginners and experienced developers through the journey of mastering full-stack JavaScript development. It takes you step-by-step through the process of building dynamic, scalable, and secure web applications using JavaScript across both the **frontend** and the **backend**.

What You Will Learn in This Book

This book is not just about learning the syntax and functionality of JavaScript. Instead, it provides a comprehensive guide to building full-fledged web applications. You will learn how to use JavaScript to develop both the **frontend** and **backend** of web applications, and how to connect them seamlessly to deliver a smooth user experience.

1. **Frontend Development with JavaScript**: The frontend of any web application is what the user interacts with. It's the part that makes the application visually appealing and functional. This book will guide you through:

- o Creating dynamic user interfaces with **HTML**, **CSS**, and **JavaScript**.

- o Leveraging modern frontend frameworks like **React**, **Vue**, and **Angular** to build interactive web applications.

- o Managing state and handling data in a way that ensures your app is responsive and smooth.

2. **Backend Development with Node.js**: While the frontend takes care of what users see and interact with, the backend powers the app with data, logic, and functionality. In this book, you will:

- o Learn how to build robust backend services using **Node.js**.

- o Understand how to interact with **databases** (both **SQL** and **NoSQL**) to store and retrieve data.

- o Build **RESTful APIs** to allow your frontend to communicate with the backend using HTTP methods like **GET**, **POST**, **PUT**, and **DELETE**.

- o Secure your applications with **JWT authentication** and **Passport.js** to handle user sessions and roles.

3. **Connecting the Frontend and Backend**: One of the critical aspects of full-stack development is the ability to seamlessly integrate the frontend with the backend. This book teaches you how to use tools like **AJAX**, **Fetch API**, and **WebSockets** to connect the frontend with your backend services.

4. **Deployment and Best Practices**: After developing your application, you'll need to deploy it to a server so that users can access it. This book covers deployment on platforms like **Heroku** for your backend and **Netlify** for your frontend. We will also

dive into industry best practices for version control using **Git, code structure**, and how to ensure the application's security and maintainability with proper **testing**.

5. **Real-World Examples and Projects**: Throughout this book, we provide hands-on examples and projects that reflect real-world use cases. Whether you're building a **blog app, social media platform**, or **e-commerce store**, the examples will guide you through the essential steps, making complex concepts simple and digestible.

Why Full-Stack JavaScript?

JavaScript is the language of the web. It runs on nearly every browser, making it the perfect choice for **frontend development**. But the world of web development is rapidly changing, and JavaScript now extends beyond the frontend.

With the rise of **Node.js**, JavaScript has become a powerful tool for backend development as well. The ability to use the same language on both sides of the application streamlines the development process and makes it easier to build full-stack applications. This means you don't have to context-switch between different programming languages or technologies, and your codebase can be more cohesive and unified.

Furthermore, JavaScript's vast ecosystem, supported by the **npm** (Node Package Manager) registry, makes it a versatile tool for developers. With tools like **Express.js**, **MongoDB**, **Passport.js**, and **React**, JavaScript can be used to build everything from simple static websites to complex, real-time applications.

Who This Book Is For

This book is intended for developers who are:

- New to full-stack development and looking to get a solid foundation in JavaScript from both the frontend and backend perspectives.

- Experienced developers looking to learn more about building modern, scalable web applications with JavaScript.

- Those interested in transitioning from frontend development to full-stack JavaScript or looking to sharpen their backend skills with **Node.js** and **Express**.

Whether you are building your first web app or are looking to expand your knowledge of full-stack JavaScript development, this book will provide you with the skills and knowledge to create modern web applications that meet the needs of users and businesses.

Why This Book Stands Out

Unlike many books that focus solely on frontend or backend technologies, this book is designed to give you a **holistic view** of full-stack development with **JavaScript**. Each chapter builds upon the last, ensuring that you not only learn how to create powerful web applications, but also understand how each part of the application fits together.

- **Comprehensive Coverage**: From setting up your development environment to deploying your final product, this book covers everything you need to know to become a proficient full-stack developer using JavaScript.

- **Real-World Applications**: All examples are designed to reflect the challenges you'll face in real-world projects, giving you practical experience.

- **Hands-on Projects**: Each chapter contains practical, hands-on examples that allow you to immediately apply what you've learned.

- **Industry Best Practices**: You will learn not just the "how," but the "why" behind the best practices in full-stack JavaScript development. This includes code organization, version control, testing, and deployment.

What You Will Achieve After Reading This Book

By the end of this book, you will have the skills and knowledge to:

- Build modern web applications using **JavaScript** across the full stack.

- Develop dynamic, responsive user interfaces using **React**, **Vue**, or **Angular**.

- Implement a robust backend with **Node.js** and **Express**, handle databases with **MongoDB** or

MySQL, and build secure authentication systems using **JWT** and **Passport.js**.

- Integrate the frontend and backend seamlessly using **AJAX**, **Fetch API**, and **WebSockets**.

- Deploy full-stack applications using platforms like **Heroku**, **Netlify**, and **AWS**.

- Implement best practices for code structure, testing, and version control to ensure your applications are maintainable, scalable, and secure.

Conclusion

As the demand for full-stack JavaScript developers continues to grow, mastering both the frontend and backend will open up a world of opportunities. This book serves as a comprehensive guide to mastering the key skills needed to build modern web applications using JavaScript.

With practical examples, real-world projects, and hands-on exercises, you will gain the expertise needed to confidently develop full-stack web applications. By the end of this journey, you will not only understand the core principles of full-stack development but also be ready to build your own powerful, production-ready applications.

Let's begin your journey into full-stack JavaScript development and start building the applications of tomorrow!

CHAPTER 1

INTRODUCTION TO JAVASCRIPT

AND WEB DEVELOPMENT

What is JavaScript and Why It's Essential in Web Development?

JavaScript is a high-level, versatile programming language primarily used to create dynamic and interactive web pages. It is a core component of web development, enabling websites to respond to user input, display real-time data, and offer rich experiences beyond static content.

JavaScript works alongside HTML (which structures the content of a webpage) and CSS (which handles the visual presentation) to add interactivity, animations, and functionality. Without JavaScript, websites would be static, with no ability to respond to actions like button clicks, form

19

submissions, or real-time data updates. It's the language that turns a webpage from something users can only look at into something they can engage with.

Why JavaScript is Important:

- **Universality:** JavaScript is the language that runs in all major web browsers, which makes it a universal tool for building web applications.

- **Interactivity:** From simple form validations to complex single-page applications (SPAs), JavaScript brings life to the web.

- **Popularity:** JavaScript is the most widely used language for web development, with massive community support, libraries, frameworks, and resources.

- **Full-Stack Capability:** With the rise of Node.js, JavaScript is no longer limited to the frontend. It's now also used for backend development, allowing you to use the same language for both the client and server sides of a web application.

Understanding Web Development: Frontend, Backend, and Full-Stack

Web development can be broadly divided into three main categories: frontend, backend, and full-stack development.

1. **Frontend Development (Client-Side):** Frontend development refers to the creation of the parts of a website or web application that users interact with directly. This includes everything from the layout, buttons, navigation menus, and forms to how these elements react when users interact with them.

   o **Languages:** HTML, CSS, and JavaScript are the primary tools for frontend development.

   o **Frameworks & Libraries:** React, Vue.js, and Angular are popular JavaScript libraries and frameworks used for building modern frontend applications.

2. **Backend Development (Server-Side):** Backend development focuses on what happens behind the scenes of a website or web application. It's responsible for managing databases, handling requests from the frontend, processing data, and ensuring that everything functions correctly.

   o **Languages:** Common backend languages include JavaScript (Node.js), Python, Ruby, Java, and PHP.

   o **Databases:** Databases like MySQL, PostgreSQL, and MongoDB store data that the backend processes and sends to the frontend.

3. **Full-Stack Development:** Full-stack developers work on both the frontend and backend of a web application, meaning they handle everything from the user interface to server-side logic and databases. Full-stack developers are highly versatile because they can build complete, end-to-end web applications.

Setting Up Your Development Environment

Before you start writing JavaScript or building web applications, it's important to set up the right development environment. The tools you use for coding, testing, and deploying your projects can have a big impact on your workflow and productivity. Here's how to get started:

1. **Code Editors:** A good code editor is essential for writing clean, error-free code. Some popular choices for JavaScript development include:

   o **Visual Studio Code (VS Code):** A free, open-source code editor with extensive JavaScript support, including debugging, linting, and integration with Git.

   o **Sublime Text:** A fast, lightweight editor with a simple interface and powerful extensions.

o **Atom:** A customizable editor that's great for web development and comes with built-in GitHub integration.

2. **Browsers:** Modern web development heavily relies on browsers for testing and debugging code. Here are some tools to get you started:

   o **Google Chrome:** With the Chrome Developer Tools (DevTools), you can inspect elements, test JavaScript, and debug issues in real-time.

   o **Firefox Developer Edition:** Offers many of the same features as Chrome DevTools, with some unique tools for JavaScript debugging.

3. **Installing Node.js:** For backend development with JavaScript, you'll need Node.js. Node.js is a runtime that allows you to run JavaScript on the server-side. Installing Node.js will also give you access to **npm** (Node Package Manager), which helps manage packages and dependencies for your project.

  o Download Node.js from the official website and follow the installation instructions for your operating system.

4. **Version Control (Git):** Git is a version control system that helps you keep track of changes in your code and collaborate with others. Set up **Git** and create an account on GitHub to start hosting your projects and collaborating with other developers.

By setting up a proper development environment, you'll be well-equipped to start writing JavaScript, building interactive websites, and working on full-stack applications. This chapter will serve as the foundation for understanding how JavaScript fits into the broader web development landscape.

CHAPTER 2

JAVASCRIPT BASICS:

VARIABLES, DATA TYPES, AND

OPERATORS

Introduction to Variables and Constants

In JavaScript, variables and constants are used to store data that you can use throughout your program. These data points can change (in the case of variables) or remain constant (in the case of constants).

1. **Variables:** Variables are used to store values that may change as your program runs. You declare variables using the `let` or `var` keywords, but `let` is preferred in modern JavaScript because it has block scope, while `var` has function scope.

Example:

javascript

```
let age = 25;  // Declaring a variable named
'age' with an initial value of 25
age = 26;        // The value of 'age' can
change to 26
```

2. **Constants:** Constants are variables whose values cannot be changed once they are assigned. You declare constants using the const keyword. If you try to reassign a constant, you'll get an error.

Example:

javascript

```
const birthYear = 1995; // Declaring a
constant 'birthYear' with a value of 1995
// birthYear = 1996; // This would cause an
error because constants can't be reassigned
```

27

Using `let` and `const` helps to make your code more predictable and easier to debug by ensuring that values either change when expected or remain the same.

Exploring Data Types: Strings, Numbers, Arrays, and Objects

JavaScript supports a variety of data types that you can use to store information. Understanding these data types is crucial to writing efficient and effective JavaScript code.

1. **Strings:** A string is a sequence of characters, such as words, sentences, or even symbols. You can create a string by enclosing characters in either single (') or double (") quotes.

   Example:

   ```javascript
   ```

```
let name = "John Doe";  // A string of text
let greeting = 'Hello, World!';  // Another
way to define a string
```

You can also use template literals (backticks `) for strings that include variables or expressions:

```
javascript
```

```
let age = 30;
let message = `Hello, I am ${age} years
old.`;  // String with embedded expression
```

2. **Numbers:** JavaScript uses numbers to represent both integers (whole numbers) and floating-point values (decimal numbers). There's no need to declare separate types for integers and floats as JavaScript handles them as the same data type.

Example:

```
javascript
```

```
let count = 42;        // An integer
let price = 19.99;     // A floating-point
number
```

You can perform arithmetic operations on numbers using operators like +, -, *, /, and %.

3. **Arrays:** An array is an ordered collection of values. Arrays can hold multiple values of different types. You define an array using square brackets [], and the values inside the array are separated by commas.

    Example:

    javascript

    ```
    let fruits = ["apple", "banana", "cherry"];
    // An array with three string elements
    let numbers = [1, 2, 3, 4];   // An array
    with numbers
    ```

You can access array items by their index, starting from 0:

```javascript
console.log(fruits[0]);    // Outputs: "apple"
```

Arrays have several useful methods like `.push()`, `.pop()`, `.shift()`, and `.unshift()` for adding or removing elements.

4. **Objects:** Objects are used to store collections of related data in the form of key-value pairs. You define an object using curly braces `{}` and separate the key-value pairs with commas. Keys are typically strings, and values can be any data type, including other objects or arrays.

   Example:

```
javascript

let person = {
    name: "Alice",
    age: 28,
    city: "New York"
};
console.log(person.name);     // Outputs:
"Alice"
```

Objects are a great way to group data that belongs together, such as a user profile with attributes like name, age, and city.

Understanding Operators: Arithmetic, Logical, and Comparison

Operators are symbols used to perform operations on values or variables. JavaScript provides a wide range of operators to manipulate and compare data.

1. **Arithmetic Operators:** These operators are used to perform mathematical calculations. The basic arithmetic operators are:

   o + (Addition)

   o - (Subtraction)

   o * (Multiplication)

   o / (Division)

   o % (Modulo or remainder)

   Example:

   javascript

```
let sum = 10 + 5;  // sum equals 15
let difference = 10 - 5;  // difference
equals 5
let product = 10 * 5;  // product equals 50
let quotient = 10 / 5;  // quotient equals
2
let remainder = 10 % 3;  // remainder equals
1
```

2. **Logical Operators:** Logical operators are used to combine multiple conditions in control flow statements. The most common logical operators are:

- o `&&` (Logical AND)
- o `||` (Logical OR)
- o `!` (Logical NOT)

Example:

javascript

```
let isAdult = true;
let hasTicket = false;
console.log(isAdult && hasTicket);   //
false, because both conditions must be true
for AND
console.log(isAdult || hasTicket);   //
true, because at least one condition is
true for OR
```

3. **Comparison Operators:** Comparison operators are used to compare values. The result is a boolean value (true or false):

    o   == (Equal to)

    o   === (Strictly equal to – checks both value and type)

    o   != (Not equal to)

    o   > (Greater than)

    o   < (Less than)

    o   >= (Greater than or equal to)

    o   <= (Less than or equal to)

    Example:

    javascript

    ```
    console.log(10 == 10);  // true
    console.log(10 === "10");   // false,
    because the types are different
    console.log(10 > 5);  // true
    console.log(10 < 5);  // false
    ```

Each operator serves a specific purpose, whether for simple arithmetic, combining conditions in an if statement, or checking if two values are equal. By understanding these basic data types and operators, you're well-equipped to start writing more complex JavaScript code!

CHAPTER 3

CONTROL FLOW AND LOOPS IN JAVASCRIPT

If/Else Statements and Conditional Logic

Conditional logic allows your program to make decisions based on specific criteria. In JavaScript, this is achieved through if, else if, and else statements. These statements evaluate conditions and execute blocks of code depending on whether those conditions are true or false.

1. **Basic If/Else Statement:** The if statement checks a condition. If the condition is true, the code block inside the if statement is executed. If the condition is false, the code block inside the else statement (if provided) is executed.

Example:

```
javascript


let age = 20;


if (age >= 18) {
    console.log("You are an adult.");
} else {
    console.log("You are a minor.");
}
```

In this example, if the age is greater than or equal to 18, the message "You are an adult" is printed. Otherwise, "You are a minor" is printed.

2. **Else If:** Sometimes, you need to check multiple conditions. This is where else if comes in handy. It lets you check another condition if the first if condition was false.

Example:

```
javascript


let temperature = 25;


if (temperature > 30) {

    console.log("It's a hot day!");

} else if (temperature > 20) {

    console.log("It's a pleasant day.");

} else {

    console.log("It's a cold day.");

}
```

This checks if the temperature is greater than 30, between 20 and 30, or less than 20, and prints the appropriate message for each case.

3. **Ternary Operator:** The ternary operator is a shorthand for `if/else` statements. It's a compact way of writing simple conditions.

Example:

```
javascript

let age = 16;
let canDrive = (age >= 18) ? "You can drive"
: "You cannot drive";
console.log(canDrive);
```

Here, if the age is 18 or greater, "You can drive" is assigned to canDrive; otherwise, "You cannot drive" is assigned.

Working with Loops: For, While, and Do-While

Loops are used to repeat a block of code multiple times. JavaScript provides several types of loops, including for, while, and do-while.

1. **For Loop:** A for loop is ideal when you know in advance how many times you want to repeat a block of code. It contains three parts:

- o **Initialization:** Sets up the loop variable.

- o **Condition:** Specifies when the loop will stop.

- o **Increment/Decrement:** Changes the loop variable after each iteration.

Example:

```javascript
for (let i = 0; i < 5; i++) {
    console.log(i);  // Prints numbers from 0 to 4
}
```

In this loop, the variable i starts at 0, the condition i < 5 is checked before each iteration, and i is incremented by 1 each time.

2. **While Loop:** A while loop keeps executing as long as the condition is true. It's useful when you don't know how many times you'll need to repeat an action

in advance, but you know the condition that will eventually stop the loop.

Example:

```javascript
let i = 0;
while (i < 5) {
    console.log(i);  // Prints numbers from 0 to 4
    i++;
}
```

The loop runs as long as the condition i < 5 is true. After each iteration, i is incremented by 1.

3. **Do-While Loop:** A do-while loop is similar to a while loop, but the condition is checked after the code block executes. This means the loop will always execute at least once, regardless of the condition.

Example:

```
javascript


let i = 0;
do {
    console.log(i);  // Prints numbers from
0 to 4
    i++;
} while (i < 5);
```

In this example, the code block runs once before the condition is evaluated. If the condition is still true, the loop will continue.

Real-World Example: Building a Simple Decision-Making App

Now that you understand control flow and loops, let's build a simple decision-making app using these concepts. The app

43

will ask the user for their age and then make a decision based on the input.

1. **Define the decision-making logic:** We will use `if/else` statements to check the user's age and print an appropriate message.

   Example code:

   ```javascript
   let age = prompt("Please enter your age:");
   // Ask for the user's age
   age = parseInt(age);   // Convert the input
   to a number

   if (age < 18) {
       console.log("You are too young to enter
   this website.");
   } else if (age >= 18 && age <= 25) {
       console.log("Welcome  to  the  website,
   young adult!");
   ```

```
} else {
    console.log("Welcome  to  the  website,
adult!");
}
```

In this example:

- o The app prompts the user for their age.
- o It then checks the age using conditional logic (`if/else`).
- o Based on the age, the app outputs an appropriate message to the user.

2. **Add loops for repeated decision-making:** If you want to allow the user to enter their age multiple times (for example, in case they make a mistake), you can use a `do-while` loop.

Example code:

```
javascript
```

```
let age;
```

45

```
do {

    age = prompt("Please enter your age:");

    age = parseInt(age);

    if (isNaN(age)) {

        console.log("Invalid input, please
enter a valid number.");

    }

} while (isNaN(age));   // Repeat until a
valid number is entered


if (age < 18) {

    console.log("You are too young to enter
this website.");

} else if (age >= 18 && age <= 25) {

    console.log("Welcome to the website,
young adult!");

} else {

    console.log("Welcome to the website,
adult!");

}
```

In this updated version:

- o The loop ensures the user inputs a valid number.

- o If the input is invalid, the app will ask the user to enter a valid number until they do so.

By using control flow statements and loops, you can build interactive and dynamic applications that respond to user input and make decisions based on specific conditions. This decision-making app is a simple example of how to apply these concepts in a real-world scenario.

CHAPTER 4

FUNCTIONS: DECLARING, CALLING, AND RETURNING VALUES

Defining Functions and Using Parameters

A function is a block of reusable code that performs a specific task. Functions can take input values (called parameters), process them, and return a result. Defining functions is one of the most powerful features of JavaScript, as it allows you to organize and reuse your code efficiently.

1. **Defining Functions:** You define a function using the `function` keyword, followed by the function name, parameters (optional), and the code block inside curly braces `{}`.

Example of a simple function definition:

```javascript
```

```javascript
function greet() {
    console.log("Hello, World!");
}
```

This function, `greet`, doesn't take any parameters and simply logs a message to the console when called.

2. **Calling Functions:** To run or invoke a function, you simply use its name followed by parentheses. If the function has parameters, you include the arguments (values) inside the parentheses.

Example:

```javascript
```

```
greet();    // Calling the greet function,
which will log "Hello, World!"
```

3. **Using Parameters:** Functions can accept parameters, which are placeholders for the values you pass when calling the function. The parameters can be used within the function to perform operations.

Example:

```javascript
function addNumbers(a, b) {
    return a + b;
}


let result = addNumbers(3, 5);   // Calling
the function with 3 and 5 as arguments
console.log(result);   // Outputs: 8
```

In this example, `a` and `b` are parameters that the function `addNumbers` uses to add two numbers together. The function then returns the result of the addition.

Understanding Function Scopes and Closures

1. **Function Scope:** Every function in JavaScript has its own scope. This means that variables declared inside a function are local to that function and are not accessible outside of it. Similarly, variables declared outside of a function are not accessible inside the function, unless passed as parameters or through global scope.

   Example of function scope:

   ```
   javascript
   ```

```
function exampleFunction() {
    let localVar = "I am local!";
    console.log(localVar);      //  Works,
because it's inside the function
}


exampleFunction();
//  console.log(localVar);     //  Error:
localVar  is  not  defined,  as  it's  not
accessible outside
```

The variable `localVar` is accessible only inside `exampleFunction()` because it's declared within the function's scope.

2. **Closures:** A closure is created when a function retains access to its lexical scope even after the function that created it has finished executing. In simpler terms, a closure allows a function to "remember" the environment in which it was created.

Example of a closure:

```javascript
function outerFunction() {
    let outerVar = "I am from outer scope!";

    function innerFunction() {
        console.log(outerVar);    // The inner function has access to outerVar
    }

    return innerFunction;  // Return the inner function as the closure
}

let closure = outerFunction();  // Call outerFunction, which returns innerFunction
closure();  // Logs: "I am from outer scope!"
```

Even though outerFunction has finished executing, the innerFunction (the closure) still has access to `outerVar`, demonstrating how closures allow functions to "remember" their environment.

Example: Building a Reusable Calculator Function

Let's combine everything we've learned about functions, parameters, scopes, and closures by building a simple reusable calculator function. The calculator will allow users to perform different operations (addition, subtraction, multiplication, division) based on their inputs.

1. **Step 1: Define the Calculator Function:**

   We'll define a function called `calculate` that takes three parameters: two numbers and an operation. The function will return the result of the specified operation.

   Example:

javascript

```javascript
function calculate(num1, num2, operation) {
    if (operation === "add") {
        return num1 + num2;
    } else if (operation === "subtract") {
        return num1 - num2;
    } else if (operation === "multiply") {
        return num1 * num2;
    } else if (operation === "divide") {
        if (num2 !== 0) {
            return num1 / num2;
        } else {
            return "Cannot divide by zero!";
        }
    } else {
        return "Invalid operation!";
    }
}
```

In this calculate function:

- o num1 and num2 are the numbers the user wants to operate on.

- o operation is a string that determines which mathematical operation to perform.

2. **Step 2: Call the Function:**

Now, we'll call the calculate function with different arguments to perform different calculations.

Example:

javascript

```
let sum = calculate(5, 3, "add");
let difference = calculate(5, 3, "subtract");
let product = calculate(5, 3, "multiply");
let quotient = calculate(5, 0, "divide");

console.log(sum);        // Outputs: 8
console.log(difference); // Outputs: 2
```

```
console.log(product);      // Outputs: 15
console.log(quotient);        //  Outputs:
"Cannot divide by zero!"
```

This simple `calculate` function is reusable, and you can pass different values and operations to it, making it flexible for various calculations.

3. **Step 3: Optional - Using Closures for Operation Selection:**

You can also use closures to build a more advanced calculator that remembers the operation to perform. For example, if you wanted a function that always adds numbers, you could use a closure to create an "add-only" calculator.

Example:

```javascript
```

```
function createAdditionCalculator() {
```

```
   return function(num1, num2) {

      return num1 + num2;

   };

}
```

```
let         addCalculator        =
createAdditionCalculator();      //   The
closure remembers "add"
console.log(addCalculator(5,  3));   //
Outputs: 8
```

The function `createAdditionCalculator` returns a new function that always adds two numbers, demonstrating how closures can be used to create specialized, reusable functions.

By mastering functions, parameters, scopes, and closures, you can write more modular, reusable, and organized code in JavaScript. Functions allow you to break down problems into smaller, manageable pieces and can be used to handle complex logic in a clean, efficient way. The reusable calculator is just one example of how functions can be applied in practical, real-world scenarios.

CHAPTER 5

OBJECTS AND ARRAYS: WORKING WITH COLLECTIONS OF DATA

Understanding Objects and Arrays in JavaScript

In JavaScript, objects and arrays are essential data structures used to store and manage collections of data. Understanding how to use and manipulate these structures is crucial to working with more complex data in your applications.

1. **Objects:** An object is a collection of key-value pairs, where each key (also called a property) is a string and the value can be any data type, including other objects or arrays. Objects are commonly used to store

data that belongs together, like user information or product details.

Creating an Object: You can create an object using curly braces {}, with each property separated by a comma.

Example:

```javascript
let person = {
    name: "Alice",
    age: 28,
    city: "New York"
};


console.log(person.name);    // Outputs: Alice
console.log(person.age);    // Outputs: 28
```

In this example, the `person` object has three properties: `name`, `age`, and `city`. You can access the values using dot notation (e.g., `person.name`).

2. **Arrays:** An array is an ordered collection of values, where each value is accessible by its index, starting from `0`. Arrays can hold multiple types of data, such as strings, numbers, objects, and even other arrays.

   Creating an Array: You can create an array using square brackets `[]`, with elements separated by commas.

   Example:

   javascript

   ```javascript
   let fruits = ["apple", "banana", "cherry"];
   console.log(fruits[0]);  // Outputs: apple
   console.log(fruits[2]);     //    Outputs: cherry
   ```

In this example, the array `fruits` holds three strings. You can access each element by its index (`fruits[0]` for "apple", `fruits[1]` for "banana", etc.).

Manipulating Objects and Arrays

Once you understand how to define objects and arrays, it's essential to know how to manipulate them — that is, how to add, remove, or modify data.

1. **Manipulating Objects:**

   o **Adding/Updating Properties:** You can add or update properties by directly assigning values using dot notation or bracket notation.

   Example:

   ```
   javascript
   ```

```
let person = {

    name: "Alice",

    age: 28

};


// Adding a new property

person.city = "New York";    // New

property 'city' added


// Updating an existing property

person.age = 29;   // Updating 'age'

property


console.log(person.city);         //

Outputs: New York

console.log(person.age);          //

Outputs: 29
```

- o **Deleting Properties:** You can delete properties using the `delete` keyword.

  Example:

```javascript
delete person.age;    // Deletes the
'age' property
console.log(person.age);         //
Outputs: undefined
```

2. **Manipulating Arrays:**

   o **Adding/Removing Elements:** You can use various methods to add or remove elements from an array.

   - **.push():** Adds elements to the end of the array.

   - **.pop():** Removes elements from the end of the array.

   - **.shift():** Removes elements from the beginning of the array.

   - **.unshift():** Adds elements to the beginning of the array.

   Example:

```javascript
javascript


let fruits = ["apple", "banana"];
fruits.push("cherry");      // Adds
"cherry" to the end
console.log(fruits);      // Outputs:
["apple", "banana", "cherry"]


fruits.pop();    // Removes the last
element ("cherry")
console.log(fruits);      // Outputs:
["apple", "banana"]


fruits.shift();  // Removes the first
element ("apple")
console.log(fruits);      // Outputs:
["banana"]


fruits.unshift("orange");    // Adds
"orange" to the beginning
console.log(fruits);              //
Outputs: ["orange", "banana"]
```

○ **Accessing and Modifying Array Elements:**
You can access and modify elements in an array using their index.

Example:

```javascript
let fruits = ["apple", "banana", "cherry"];
fruits[1] = "blueberry"; // Changes "banana" to "blueberry"
console.log(fruits); // Outputs: ["apple", "blueberry", "cherry"]
```

Example: Building a To-Do List App with Arrays and Objects

Now that we've covered objects and arrays, let's build a simple to-do list app. This app will allow users to add tasks, mark them as complete, and display the tasks.

1. **Step 1: Define the Task Structure (Object):** Each task will be an object with properties such as `title` (the task description) and `completed` (a boolean value indicating whether the task is completed or not).

   Example:

   ```javascript
   javascript

   let tasks = [
       { title: "Buy groceries", completed: false },
       { title: "Walk the dog", completed: false }
   ];
   ```

2. **Step 2: Add a Task Function:** Create a function to add a new task to the list. The function will accept the task's title and create a new object with the title and a default `completed` value of `false`.

Example:

```javascript
function addTask(title) {
    tasks.push({ title: title, completed: false });
}

addTask("Clean the house");  // Adds a new task to the array
console.log(tasks);
```

3. **Step 3: Mark Task as Complete:** Create a function to mark a task as complete. This function will find

the task by its index and update the `completed` property to `true`.

Example:

```
javascript
```

```javascript
function completeTask(index) {
    if (tasks[index]) {
        tasks[index].completed = true;
    }
}

completeTask(0);   // Marks the first task
as completed
console.log(tasks);
```

4. **Step 4: Display Tasks:** Create a function that loops through the `tasks` array and prints each task, including whether it's completed or not.

Example:

```
javascript

function displayTasks() {
    tasks.forEach((task, index) => {
        console.log(`${index    +    1}.
${task.title}    -    ${task.completed    ?
"Completed" : "Incomplete"}`);
    });
}

displayTasks();
```

5. **Step 5: Put it All Together:** Let's combine all the parts into a simple to-do list app.

Example:

```
javascript

let tasks = [
    { title: "Buy groceries", completed:
false },
```

```
  { title: "Walk the dog", completed:
false }
];


function addTask(title) {
    tasks.push({ title: title, completed:
false });
}


function completeTask(index) {
    if (tasks[index]) {
        tasks[index].completed = true;
    }
}


function displayTasks() {
    tasks.forEach((task, index) => {
        console.log(`${index + 1}.
${task.title} - ${task.completed ?
"Completed" : "Incomplete"}`);
    });
}
```

```
addTask("Clean the house");

completeTask(0);

displayTasks();  // Outputs: Task list with

one completed task
```

This simple to-do list app demonstrates how to use objects to store task details and arrays to manage the collection of tasks. By understanding how to manipulate both objects and arrays, you can create more complex applications to handle various types of data.

CHAPTER 6

DOM MANIPULATION:

INTERACTING WITH WEB PAGES

What is the DOM (Document Object Model)?

The DOM (Document Object Model) is a programming interface for web documents. It represents the structure of a webpage as a tree of objects, where each object corresponds to a part of the webpage, such as an element, an attribute, or even text content. The DOM allows developers to interact with the content, structure, and style of a webpage using JavaScript.

Think of the DOM as a map of your webpage. Every element (like a `div`, `p`, `button`, etc.) is an object in the DOM, and JavaScript allows you to manipulate these objects in real-time to create dynamic, interactive websites.

Key Concepts:

- **Elements**: HTML tags, such as `<div>`, `<h1>`, `<p>`, etc.

- **Attributes**: Properties of elements, such as `id`, `class`, `src`, etc.

- **Text Content**: The textual data inside elements, like paragraphs or headings.

Interacting with the DOM Using JavaScript: Using JavaScript, you can select elements, modify their properties, or even remove them from the webpage. This allows you to build interactive features like buttons that change text, forms that show or hide elements, or dynamic content updates.

Selecting, Modifying, and Removing Elements on a Webpage

1. **Selecting   Elements**:
   JavaScript provides various methods to select HTML

elements from the DOM. The most common methods are:

- o document.getElementById(): Selects an element by its id.

- o document.getElementsByClassName(): Selects elements by their class name.

- o document.querySelector(): Selects the first element that matches a CSS selector.

- o document.querySelectorAll(): Selects all elements that match a CSS selector.

Examples:

javascript

```
let             heading            =
document.getElementById("main-heading");
// Select element by id
let             buttons            =
document.getElementsByClassName("btn");
// Select elements by class
```

```
let            firstParagraph            =
document.querySelector("p");    // Select
the first <p> element
```

2. **Modifying   Elements**:

   After selecting an element, you can change its content or attributes. Common operations include:

   - **Changing   text   content**: `element.textContent`   or `element.innerHTML`.

   - **Changing   HTML   attributes**: `element.setAttribute()`   or   directly modifying the property.

   - **Changing styles**: Modifying CSS properties using `element.style`.

   Examples:

   ```
   javascript
   ```

   ```
   // Change text content
   ```

```
heading.textContent = "Welcome to My
Website!"; // Changes the text inside the
heading


// Change an attribute (e.g., an image's
source)
let image = document.querySelector("img");
image.setAttribute("src", "new-
image.jpg");


// Modify CSS styles
heading.style.color = "blue"; // Changes
the text color of the heading
```

3. **Removing Elements**:

To remove an element from the webpage, you can use the `remove()` method or `parentElement.removeChild()` if you need more control.

Examples:

```javascript

// Directly remove an element
let button = document.querySelector("button");
button.remove();   // Removes the button from the page


// Remove an element using its parent
let container = document.querySelector(".container");
let itemToRemove = document.querySelector(".item");
container.removeChild(itemToRemove);   // Removes an item from the container
```

Example: Creating an Interactive Form with JavaScript

Let's build a simple interactive form using the DOM to demonstrate how you can manipulate elements on a webpage based on user input. We will create a form where users can enter their name, and once they click a button, their name will be displayed in a greeting message.

Step 1: HTML Structure

html

```
<!DOCTYPE html>
<html lang="en">
<head>
    <meta charset="UTF-8">
    <meta name="viewport" content="width=device-width, initial-scale=1.0">
    <title>Interactive Form</title>
</head>
<body>

    <h1>Welcome to Our Website</h1>

    <form id="name-form">
        <label for="name">Enter your name:</label>
```

```
    <input type="text" id="name" name="name"
required>
        <button    type="submit"     id="submit-
btn">Submit</button>
    </form>


    <p id="greeting-message"></p>


    <script src="script.js"></script>

</body>
</html>
```

Step 2: JavaScript to Handle Interactions

In the script.js file, we will add functionality to the form. When the user submits the form, the inputted name will appear in a greeting message below the form.

```
javascript


// Select elements from the DOM
```

```javascript
const form = document.getElementById("name-form");
const nameInput = document.getElementById("name");
const greetingMessage = document.getElementById("greeting-message");
const submitButton = document.getElementById("submit-btn");

// Add event listener for form submission
form.addEventListener("submit", function(event) {
    event.preventDefault(); // Prevent the form from submitting and reloading the page

    let name = nameInput.value; // Get the value from the input field

    // Modify the greeting message
    if (name.trim() !== "") {
        greetingMessage.textContent = `Hello, ${name}! Welcome to our website.`;
```

```
    } else {

        greetingMessage.textContent  =  "Please
enter your name.";

    }


    // Clear the input field after submission
    nameInput.value = "";
});
```

Step 3: Explanation of the JavaScript

1. **Selecting   Elements**:

   We use `document.getElementById()` to select the

   form, input field, and the paragraph where the

   greeting message will appear.

2. **Event   Listener   for   Form   Submission**:

   We add an event listener to the form that listens for

   the `submit` event. When the user submits the form,

   the event handler prevents the form from submitting

   (which would reload the page) by calling

   `event.preventDefault()`.

83

3. **Handling the Input Value**: We get the value entered by the user using `nameInput.value`. If the user has entered something, the message updates to greet the user. If the input is empty, the message asks the user to enter their name.

4. **Clearing the Input Field**: After the form is submitted, we clear the input field to prepare it for the next submission.

Step 4: Result

When the user enters their name and clicks the submit button, the form will display a personalized greeting below it.

This example demonstrates how to interact with the DOM to create a simple, dynamic web experience. By selecting elements, modifying content, and adding event listeners, you

can create interactive, user-friendly webpages.

CHAPTER 7

EVENT HANDLING: MAKING WEB PAGES INTERACTIVE

Understanding Events (Click, Input, Change, etc.)

In web development, events are actions or occurrences that happen in the system you are working with. These actions can be initiated by the user (like clicking a button or typing in a text field) or by the browser (such as when a page finishes loading). Event handling allows you to create interactive web pages by responding to these actions.

Common events in JavaScript include:

1. **Click**: Triggered when a user clicks on an element, such as a button or an image.

2. **Input**: Triggered when a user types or interacts with an input field.

3. **Change**: Triggered when the value of a form element (like a dropdown or a checkbox) changes.

4. **Submit**: Triggered when a form is submitted.

5. **Mouseover**: Triggered when a mouse pointer hovers over an element.

6. **Keydown/Keyup**: Triggered when a key is pressed or released.

Events allow us to control the user experience by executing specific actions in response to these events.

Adding Event Listeners and Responding to User Actions

To respond to events in JavaScript, we use **event listeners**. An event listener is a function that waits for a specific event to happen on a particular element. When the event occurs, the listener function is called, and you can perform any desired action within it.

You can add event listeners using the `addEventListener()` method. This method takes two arguments:

1. The type of event (e.g., `"click"`, `"input"`, `"change"`).

2. The callback function to execute when the event occurs.

Syntax:

```javascript
```

```javascript
element.addEventListener('event', function);
```

Example:

```javascript
```

```javascript
let button = document.getElementById('my-button');
button.addEventListener('click', function() {
    alert('Button clicked!');
});
```

In this example, when the user clicks the button, an alert with the message "Button clicked!" will pop up.

Example: Building a Dynamic Image Gallery

Now let's build an interactive image gallery that responds to user actions like clicking on thumbnails to view the full-size image. We'll use event listeners to make this gallery dynamic.

Step 1: HTML Structure

We'll start by creating the basic HTML for the gallery. We'll have a series of thumbnail images, and when clicked, they will display a larger version of the image.

```html
html
```

```html
<!DOCTYPE html>
<html lang="en">
```

```html
<head>

    <meta charset="UTF-8">

    <meta name="viewport" content="width=device-
width, initial-scale=1.0">

    <title>Dynamic Image Gallery</title>

    <style>

        .gallery {

            display: flex;

            gap: 10px;

        }


        .thumbnail {

            width: 100px;

            height: 100px;

            cursor: pointer;

            object-fit: cover;

        }


        #full-image {

            width: 500px;

            height: 500px;

            margin-top: 20px;
```

```
        }
    </style>
</head>
<body>

<h1>Dynamic Image Gallery</h1>

<div class="gallery">
    <img              src="image1-thumbnail.jpg"
class="thumbnail"     alt="Image    1"      data-
full="image1.jpg">
    <img              src="image2-thumbnail.jpg"
class="thumbnail"     alt="Image    2"      data-
full="image2.jpg">
    <img              src="image3-thumbnail.jpg"
class="thumbnail"     alt="Image    3"      data-
full="image3.jpg">
</div>

<img  id="full-image"  src=""  alt="Click  on  a
thumbnail to view the full image">
```

```
<script src="script.js"></script>


</body>

</html>
```

In this structure:

- We have three thumbnail images inside a `div` with the class `gallery`.

- Each image has a `data-full` attribute, which holds the full-size image URL that corresponds to that thumbnail.

- We have an empty `img` tag (`#full-image`) where the selected full-size image will be displayed.

Step 2: JavaScript to Handle Events

Next, we'll write the JavaScript to make the images interactive. We'll add event listeners to the thumbnails, so when a user clicks on one, it will display the full-size image.

```
javascript
```

```javascript
// Select all thumbnail images
let                    thumbnails                =
document.querySelectorAll('.thumbnail');


// Select the full image element where the
clicked image will be displayed
let fullImage = document.getElementById('full-
image');


// Add a click event listener to each thumbnail
thumbnails.forEach(function(thumbnail) {
    thumbnail.addEventListener('click',
function() {
        // Get the full-size image URL from the
data-full attribute
        let             fullImageUrl            =
thumbnail.getAttribute('data-full');


        // Change the src attribute of the full
image to the selected image's URL
        fullImage.src = fullImageUrl;
    });
```

```
});
```

Step 3: Explanation of the Code

1. **Selecting   Elements**:
   We   use
   `document.querySelectorAll('.thumbnail')` to
   select all images with the class `thumbnail`. We also
   select the `full-image` element where the larger
   version of the image will be displayed.

2. **Adding   Event   Listeners**:
   We loop through each thumbnail and add a `click`
   event listener to it. The event listener will trigger the
   callback function when the user clicks on a
   thumbnail.

3. **Updating   the   Full   Image**:
   When a thumbnail is clicked, we retrieve the full-size
   image URL from the `data-full` attribute using
   `getAttribute('data-full')`. We then update the

`src` of the `full-image` element to display the corresponding full-size image.

Step 4: Result

When you run this code and click on any of the thumbnails, the full-size version of the image will appear below the thumbnails. This simple interaction demonstrates how JavaScript event handling can be used to make a webpage dynamic and responsive to user actions.

This example shows how to use event handling to create a dynamic and interactive image gallery. By listening for click events on the thumbnail images, you can update the content of the webpage without needing to reload it, which is a key feature of modern web development.

CHAPTER 8

JAVASCRIPT ES6 FEATURES: LET, CONST, ARROW FUNCTIONS, AND MORE

Exploring the New Features Introduced in ES6

ES6, also known as ECMAScript 2015, introduced several new features to JavaScript, making the language more powerful, easier to use, and more efficient. These features include `let` and `const` for variable declarations, arrow functions for cleaner function syntax, template literals for easier string manipulation, and destructuring for simplified object and array unpacking.

---

1. Let and Const

Before ES6, JavaScript used `var` to declare variables. However, `var` had some issues, such as allowing variable redeclarations and being function-scoped. ES6 introduced `let` and `const`, which solve some of the problems associated with `var`.

- **let**: Declares a block-scoped variable, meaning the variable is only accessible within the block, statement, or expression where it is declared.

  Example:

  javascript

  ```
  let age = 25;
  if (true) {
      let age = 30;  // This age is different
  from the outer scope
      console.log(age);  // Outputs: 30
  }
  console.log(age);  // Outputs: 25
  ```

- **const**: Declares a block-scoped, read-only constant. Once assigned, the value of a const variable cannot be changed.

  Example:

  ```javascript
  const name = "Alice";
  // name = "Bob";   // Error: Assignment to constant variable.
  console.log(name);   // Outputs: Alice
  ```

- let and const are preferred over var because they provide better scoping rules and prevent accidental redeclarations.

---

2. Arrow Functions

Arrow functions provide a more concise syntax for writing functions in JavaScript. They also handle the `this` keyword differently, making them particularly useful in certain situations, like when working with callbacks or array methods.

- **Syntax**: Arrow functions use the `=>` syntax.

  Example:

  javascript

  ```javascript
  // Traditional function
  function add(a, b) {
      return a + b;
  }


  // Arrow function
  const add = (a, b) => a + b;


  console.log(add(5, 3));  // Outputs: 8
  ```

Key Benefits of Arrow Functions:

- o Concise syntax.

- o No need for the `return` keyword when there's a single expression (implicit return).

- o No binding of `this`, which means the value of `this` is inherited from the surrounding context.

Example of arrow function with `this`:

javascript

```
function Timer() {
    this.seconds = 0;
    setInterval(() => {
        this.seconds++;  // Arrow function
keeps the value of 'this' referring to the
Timer instance
        console.log(this.seconds);
    }, 1000);
}
```

```
let myTimer = new Timer();
```

3. Template Literals

Template literals provide a more readable and convenient way to work with strings. They allow embedding expressions within strings using ${} syntax and are created using backticks (`) instead of regular quotes.

- **Syntax**:

```javascript
const name = "Alice";
const greeting = `Hello, ${name}!`;  // Using template literals for string interpolation
console.log(greeting);  // Outputs: Hello, Alice!
```

- You can also use template literals to create multi-line strings:

Example:

```javascript

const message = `This is a
multi-line string
using template literals.`;
console.log(message);
```

4. Destructuring

Destructuring is a shorthand for extracting values from arrays or objects and assigning them to variables in a more concise manner.

- **Array Destructuring**:

```javascript
```

```
const colors = ["red", "blue", "green"];
const [firstColor, secondColor] = colors;


console.log(firstColor);   // Outputs: red
console.log(secondColor);      //   Outputs:
blue
```

- **Object Destructuring**:

  javascript

```
const person = { name: "Alice", age: 25,
city: "New York" };
const { name, age } = person;


console.log(name);   // Outputs: Alice
console.log(age);   // Outputs: 25
```

- Destructuring can also be used with default values and renaming variables:

  Example:

```javascript
```

```javascript
const person = { name: "Alice", age: 25 };
const { name, city = "Unknown" } = person;

console.log(name);  // Outputs: Alice
console.log(city);   // Outputs: Unknown
(default value)
```

Example: Refactoring Old Code to Use ES6 Features

Let's take some older JavaScript code and refactor it to use the new ES6 features. We'll rewrite a simple function that calculates the area of a rectangle and logs the result.

Old Code (Before ES6):

```javascript
```

```javascript
var length = 10;
var width = 5;
```

```
function calculateArea(length, width) {

    return length * width;

}
```

```
var area = calculateArea(length, width);
console.log("Area: " + area);
```

Refactored Code (Using ES6 Features):

```
javascript
```

```
const length = 10;  // Use const since the value
won't change
const width = 5;    // Same for width
```

```
// Arrow function for conciseness
const calculateArea = (length, width) => length
* width;
```

```
const area = calculateArea(length, width);
console.log(`Area: ${area}`);  // Use template
literals for cleaner string formatting
```

Breakdown of Changes:

1. **Using `const`**: We replaced `var` with `const` because the values of `length` and `width` won't change.

2. **Arrow Function**: We refactored the `calculateArea` function to use an arrow function for cleaner syntax.

3. **Template Literals**: We replaced string concatenation with a template literal for better readability when logging the result.

Conclusion

ES6 introduced many new features that enhance the readability, efficiency, and maintainability of JavaScript code. By using features like `let` and `const`, arrow functions, template literals, and destructuring, developers can write cleaner, more modern JavaScript that's easier to understand and work with. Refactoring older code to use ES6 features can significantly improve your codebase, making it more concise and less error-prone.

CHAPTER 9

ASYNCHRONOUS JAVASCRIPT: CALLBACKS, PROMISES, AND ASYNC/AWAIT

Understanding Synchronous vs Asynchronous Code

In JavaScript, synchronous and asynchronous code determine how tasks are executed in relation to one another.

1. **Synchronous Code**: Synchronous code is executed one step at a time, in the order that it appears. Each task waits for the previous one to complete before starting.

   Example of synchronous code:

   ```javascript
   ```

```
console.log("First task");
console.log("Second task");
console.log("Third task");
```

Output:

```
sql
```

```
First task
Second task
Third task
```

In this case, each log message is printed sequentially, one after the other.

2. **Asynchronous Code**: Asynchronous code allows tasks to run in the background, meaning that the program doesn't wait for one task to complete before moving on to the next. This is crucial for handling operations like file reading, database queries, and network requests, which might take time to complete.

Example of asynchronous code (using `setTimeout`):

```javascript
```

```javascript
console.log("First task");
setTimeout(() => {
    console.log("Delayed task");
}, 2000);
console.log("Second task");
```

Output:

```sql
```

```
First task
Second task
Delayed task
```

Notice that even though `setTimeout` is used to delay the second log, the program doesn't wait for it. It continues to execute the `Second task` while the delayed task is being processed in the background.

Using Callbacks, Promises, and Async/Await for Handling Asynchronous Tasks

Handling asynchronous tasks efficiently is one of the key challenges in JavaScript. We can use three primary techniques to handle async operations: **callbacks, promises**, and **async/await**.

1. Callbacks

A callback is a function passed into another function as an argument that is executed after a certain task completes. While callbacks are a simple way to handle asynchronous operations, they can sometimes lead to "callback hell," where functions are nested within each other, making the code hard to read and maintain.

Example of a callback:

```javascript
javascript


function fetchData(callback) {
    setTimeout(() => {
        const data = "Data fetched";
        callback(data);    // Call the callback
function once the task is complete
    }, 2000);
}


fetchData((data) => {
    console.log(data);   // Outputs: Data fetched
after 2 seconds
});
```

In this example, `fetchData` simulates fetching data asynchronously, and once the data is available, it calls the provided callback function with the result.

2. Promises

A **promise** is an object that represents the eventual completion (or failure) of an asynchronous operation. Promises allow you to handle asynchronous operations more cleanly and avoid the nesting issues of callbacks.

Promises have three possible states:

- **Pending**: The operation is still ongoing.
- **Resolved (Fulfilled)**: The operation completed successfully.
- **Rejected**: The operation failed.

You can handle the success or failure of a promise using `.then()` and `.catch()`.

Example of using a promise:

```javascript

function fetchData() {
    return new Promise((resolve, reject) => {
        setTimeout(() => {
```

```
        const success = true;

        if (success) {

            resolve("Data              fetched
successfully");

        } else {

            reject("Failed to fetch data");

        }

    }, 2000);

  });

}


fetchData()

  .then((data) => {

    console.log(data);    // Outputs: Data
fetched successfully

  })

  .catch((error) => {

    console.log(error);   // Outputs: Failed
to fetch data (if there's an error)

  });
```

In this example, `fetchData` returns a promise. If the operation is successful, it resolves the promise with `"Data fetched successfully"`, otherwise it rejects the promise with an error message.

3. Async/Await

`async` and `await` are built-in JavaScript keywords that simplify working with promises. An `async` function always returns a promise, and within an `async` function, you can use `await` to pause the execution of code until the promise is resolved or rejected.

`await` can only be used inside an `async` function.

Example using async/await:

```javascript
async function fetchData() {
```

```
    const  data  =  await  new  Promise((resolve,
reject) => {

        setTimeout(() => {

            const success = true;

            if (success) {

                resolve("Data                fetched
successfully");

            } else {

                reject("Failed to fetch data");

            }

        }, 2000);

    });


    console.log(data);   // Outputs: Data fetched
successfully

}


fetchData();
```

In this example, the `await` keyword pauses the execution of the function until the promise resolves, making the code look synchronous, even though it's performing asynchronous operations in the background.

Example: Fetching Data from an API

Now, let's put all of this together with a real-world example. We'll fetch data from a simulated API using both callbacks, promises, and async/await to demonstrate how these techniques work in practice.

Using a Callback to Fetch Data:

javascript

```javascript
function fetchData(callback) {
    setTimeout(() => {
        const data = { id: 1, name: "Alice" };
        callback(data);
    }, 2000);
}
```

```
fetchData((data) => {

    console.log("Callback:", data);   // Outputs:
Callback: { id: 1, name: 'Alice' }

});
```

Using a Promise to Fetch Data:

javascript

```
function fetchData() {

    return new Promise((resolve) => {

        setTimeout(() => {

            const data = { id: 1, name: "Alice"
};

            resolve(data);

        }, 2000);

    });

}


fetchData()

    .then((data) => {
```

```
    console.log("Promise:",  data);      //
Outputs: Promise: { id: 1, name: 'Alice' }
    });
```

Using Async/Await to Fetch Data:

javascript

```
async function fetchData() {
    const data = await new Promise((resolve) =>
{
        setTimeout(() => {
            const data = { id: 1, name: "Alice"
};
            resolve(data);
        }, 2000);
    });


    console.log("Async/Await:",  data);      //
Outputs: Async/Await: { id: 1, name: 'Alice' }
}


fetchData();
```

Conclusion

Asynchronous JavaScript allows you to handle time-consuming tasks, like API requests or file reading, without blocking the execution of the rest of your program. Using callbacks, promises, and async/await, you can manage asynchronous code more efficiently. `async` and `await` are particularly useful for writing clean, readable code that looks synchronous but runs asynchronously in the background, making your applications more responsive.

CHAPTER 10

FRONTEND FRAMEWORKS OVERVIEW: REACT, VUE, AND ANGULAR

Introduction to Frontend Frameworks

Frontend frameworks are collections of pre-written code that help developers build web applications more efficiently. These frameworks provide ready-made tools, libraries, and structures to manage everything from UI components to data management and routing. Instead of writing everything from scratch, developers can use these frameworks to speed up development while maintaining consistency and scalability.

The three most popular frontend frameworks today are **React**, **Vue**, and **Angular**. They each offer different features, benefits, and approaches to building modern web applications.

When to Choose React, Vue, or Angular

While all three frameworks serve the same general purpose of building user interfaces for web applications, they differ in terms of complexity, learning curve, community support, and specific use cases. Let's take a closer look at each framework to help you decide which one might be the best fit for your project.

1. **React**:
    - **Developer**: Created by Facebook (now Meta) and maintained by a large community of developers.
    - **Key Features**:
        - **Component-based architecture**: React is built around reusable components,

making it easy to manage and maintain complex UIs.

- **Declarative UI**: React allows developers to describe what the UI should look like based on the state, and it automatically handles UI updates when the state changes.

- **Virtual DOM**: React uses a virtual DOM, which improves performance by only updating the parts of the DOM that have changed.

- **Flexibility**: React provides a flexible, minimalist core, allowing developers to choose additional libraries for routing, state management, etc.

o **When to Use React**:

- Ideal for building dynamic, data-driven applications with a lot of user interaction.

- Great choice for single-page applications (SPAs) or applications with high user engagement.

- If you need flexibility and are comfortable selecting additional libraries for routing and state management (e.g., React Router, Redux).

- Well-suited for large-scale applications with complex UIs.

  o **Learning Curve**: Moderate to high, due to its flexibility and need for understanding concepts like JSX, hooks, and state management.

2. **Vue**:

   o **Developer**: Created by Evan You, a former Google engineer, and maintained by a community of developers.

   o **Key Features**:

     - **Progressive framework**: Vue is designed to be incrementally adoptable. You can use it as a simple library for UI enhancements or as a full-fledged framework for building entire applications.

- **Declarative rendering**: Similar to React, Vue uses a declarative approach to define the UI based on the application state.

- **Two-way data binding**: Vue offers two-way data binding, making it easier to manage form inputs and other user interactions.

- **Simpler setup and integration**: Vue is easier to integrate into existing projects and has a less complex setup process than Angular or React.

o **When to Use Vue**:

- Ideal for smaller projects or adding interactivity to existing websites.

125

- A good choice if you're looking for a lightweight and flexible framework with an easier learning curve.

- Great for building SPAs or simple applications with moderate complexity.

- If you value simplicity, clear documentation, and ease of use.

  o **Learning Curve**: Low to moderate, especially for developers familiar with HTML, CSS, and JavaScript. Vue's clear and concise documentation makes it beginner-friendly.

3. **Angular**:

  o **Developer**: Created and maintained by Google.

  o **Key Features**:

    - **Full-fledged framework**: Angular is a complete solution for building single-page applications. It comes with built-in features for routing, state management, and form validation, making it a "batteries-included" framework.

- **Component-based architecture**: Like React and Vue, Angular uses a component-based approach for building UIs.

- **Two-way data binding**: Angular also offers two-way data binding, simplifying the management of form inputs and other interactions.

- **TypeScript support**: Angular is built using TypeScript, a statically typed superset of JavaScript, which can improve development productivity and help catch errors early.

o **When to Use Angular**:

- Ideal for large-scale, enterprise-level applications with complex functionality.

- Best suited for projects that need an all-in-one solution, where routing, state management, and form validation are required out-of-the-box.

127

- If you prefer working with TypeScript and need built-in solutions for many common development challenges.

  o **Learning Curve**: High, due to its comprehensive feature set, the need to understand TypeScript, and its complex tooling and configurations.

Example: Setting Up a Basic React App

Let's now walk through the process of setting up a basic React app. We will use **Create React App**, a tool that helps set up a new React project with all the necessary build configurations and dependencies.

Step 1: Install Node.js and NPM

To get started with React, you need **Node.js** and **npm** (Node Package Manager) installed on your system. You can download and install them from the official website: https://nodejs.org.

Step 2: Install Create React App

Once Node.js and npm are installed, open your terminal (or command prompt) and run the following command to install `create-react-app`, a tool that helps you set up a React project:

```bash
```

```
npx create-react-app my-app
```

This command will create a new directory called `my-app` and set up a new React project in that directory with all the required files and dependencies.

Step 3: Navigate to Your Project Folder

Change your directory to the newly created `my-app` folder:

```bash
```

```
cd my-app
```

Step 4: Start the Development Server

Now, start the React development server by running the following command:

```bash
```

```
npm start
```

This will open a development server in your browser, and you should see the default React welcome screen (a spinning React logo and some welcome text).

Step 5: Edit the App Component

Now, let's modify the default React app. Open the src/App.js file in your text editor and update it with the following code:

```
javascript

import React from 'react';
import './App.css';

function App() {
  return (
    <div className="App">
      <h1>Hello, React!</h1>
      <p>This is a basic React app.</p>
    </div>
  );
}

export default App;
```

This code defines a functional component that displays a heading and a paragraph. Save the file.

Step 6: View Changes in the Browser

Once you save the changes, the React development server will automatically reload the page in the browser to reflect your changes. You should now see the updated content ("Hello, React!" and "This is a basic React app.").

Conclusion

- **React** is ideal for building dynamic, data-driven applications with complex UIs, and its component-based structure makes it easy to break down applications into manageable parts.
- **Vue** is a great option for small to medium-sized projects, especially when you need simplicity, flexibility, and a low learning curve.
- **Angular** is a complete framework that's well-suited for large-scale enterprise applications and when you want a full set of built-in tools and TypeScript support.

By understanding the differences between React, Vue, and Angular, and knowing when to choose each, you can make informed decisions that align with the needs of your project.

CHAPTER 11

BUILDING WITH REACT: COMPONENTS, STATE, AND PROPS

Introduction to React Components and JSX

React is built around components. A **component** is a reusable, self-contained unit of code that represents a part of your UI. Components allow you to break down your UI into smaller, manageable pieces, making it easier to build and maintain large applications.

- **Functional Components**: These are the simpler components that are written as JavaScript functions. They receive input via `props` and return JSX to render the UI.
- **Class Components**: These are more complex and are written as ES6 classes. They support lifecycle methods

and state management. While functional components are now the preferred way of writing components in React (especially with the introduction of hooks), understanding class components is still valuable.

JSX (JavaScript XML) is a syntax extension for JavaScript. It allows you to write HTML-like code within your JavaScript files. React uses JSX to describe what the UI should look like. JSX is then transformed into regular JavaScript code behind the scenes.

JSX Example:

jsx

```
const element = <h1>Hello, world!</h1>;
```

This JSX code will render an h1 tag with the text "Hello, world!" when placed inside a React component.

Managing State and Props in React

- **Props (short for properties)**: Props are used to pass data from a parent component to a child component. They are read-only and cannot be modified by the child component.

  Example:

  jsx

  ```
  function Greeting(props) {
      return <h1>Hello, {props.name}!</h1>;
  }


  // In a parent component:
  <Greeting name="Alice" />
  ```

  In this example, the Greeting component receives the name prop and uses it to render the greeting message. The parent component provides the name value.

- **State**: State is used to manage dynamic data within a component. Unlike props, state is mutable, meaning it can be updated over time, and changes to the state will trigger a re-render of the component.

State is usually defined inside a component using the useState hook (for functional components) or in the constructor (for class components).

Example of using state in a functional component with the useState hook:

jsx

```
import React, { useState } from 'react';

function Counter() {
    const [count, setCount] = useState(0);
// Initializes state with a value of 0

    return (
```

```
<div>
    <p>You      clicked      {count}
times</p>
    <button      onClick={()      =>
setCount(count + 1)}>Click me</button>
    </div>
  );
}


export default Counter;
```

In this example, the `Counter` component has a state variable `count`, which starts at `0`. When the button is clicked, the state is updated using the `setCount` function, and the component re-renders to reflect the new count.

Example: Building a Simple Weather App with React

Now that we understand the basics of components, state, and props, let's build a simple weather app using React. The app will allow the user to input a city and display the current weather for that city by fetching data from a weather API.

Step 1: Setting Up the React App

First, create a new React app using **Create React App**:

bash

```
npx create-react-app weather-app
cd weather-app
npm start
```

This will set up a new React project and run the development server.

Step 2: Installing Axios for API Requests

We'll use **Axios**, a promise-based HTTP client, to fetch weather data from a weather API.

Install Axios by running:

```bash
npm install axios
```

Step 3: Building the Weather Component

Now, let's build the Weather component. This component will allow the user to enter a city name, fetch weather data for that city, and display it on the page.

Edit src/App.js:

```jsx
import React, { useState } from 'react';
import axios from 'axios';
import './App.css';

function App() {
  const [city, setCity] = useState("");  // State
to store the city name
```

```javascript
const [weather, setWeather] = useState(null);
// State to store the weather data
const [error, setError] = useState("");   //
State to handle errors


const fetchWeather = () => {
  const apiKey = 'YOUR_API_KEY';   // Use your
OpenWeatherMap API key
  const apiUrl                 =
`https://api.openweathermap.org/data/2.5/weathe
r?q=${city}&appid=${apiKey}&units=metric`;


  axios.get(apiUrl)
    .then((response) => {
      setWeather(response.data);      //  Store
weather data in state
      setError("");   // Reset any previous
error messages
    })
    .catch((err) => {
      setWeather(null);    // Clear previous
weather data
```

```
    setError("City  not  found.  Please  try
again.");
    });
  };


  return (
    <div className="App">
      <h1>Weather App</h1>
      <input
        type="text"
        placeholder="Enter city"
        value={city}
        onChange={(e)                      =>
setCity(e.target.value)}  // Update city state on
input change
      />
      <button        onClick={fetchWeather}>Get
Weather</button>

      {error && <p>{error}</p>}


      {weather && (
```

```
    <div>

        <h2>Weather in {weather.name}</h2>

        <p>Temperature:
{weather.main.temp}°C</p>

        <p>Weather:
{weather.weather[0].description}</p>

        <p>Humidity:
{weather.main.humidity}%</p>

    </div>

    )}

  </div>

  );

}


export default App;
```

Step 4: Explanation of the Code

1. **State Management**:

   o   `city`: Holds the city name entered by the user.

   o   `weather`: Stores the weather data fetched from

       the API.

o   `error`: Holds any error message, for instance, when the city is not found.

2. **Fetching Weather Data**:

o   When the user clicks the "Get Weather" button, the `fetchWeather` function is called.

o   This function makes an Axios request to the OpenWeatherMap API with the city name.

o   If the request is successful, the weather data is stored in the `weather` state.

o   If an error occurs (e.g., the city is not found), the `error` state is updated with an error message.

3. **Displaying Data**:

o   If there is an error, it is displayed on the screen.

o   If the weather data is fetched successfully, it is displayed: city name, temperature, weather description, and humidity.

Step 5: Running the App

Now, when you run your app (`npm start`), you will see a basic weather app where the user can input a city, click "Get Weather," and see the temperature and weather description for that city.

Conclusion

This example demonstrates how React components work, how to manage state with `useState`, and how to pass data into components through props. Additionally, we used Axios to handle API requests, showing how React can easily integrate with external APIs. With React, you can create dynamic, responsive UIs that update automatically when the state changes, making it ideal for building interactive web applications like this weather app.

CHAPTER 12

ADVANCED REACT: HOOKS AND CONTEXT API

Understanding React Hooks: useState, useEffect, Custom Hooks

React hooks were introduced in React 16.8 to allow functional components to manage state and side effects without needing class components. Hooks are functions that let you "hook into" React features. The two most commonly used hooks are `useState` and `useEffect`, but there are others like `useContext`, `useReducer`, and custom hooks.

---

1. `useState` Hook

The **useState** hook is used to add state to functional components. It returns an array with two elements:

1. The current state value.

2. A function to update that state.

Syntax:

```javascript
const [state, setState] = useState(initialValue);
```

Example:

```javascript
import React, { useState } from 'react';

function Counter() {
  const [count, setCount] = useState(0); // Initialize state with 0
```

```
  return (

    <div>

      <p>Count: {count}</p>

      <button onClick={() => setCount(count +
1)}>Increment</button>

    </div>

  );

}
```

```
export default Counter;
```

In this example, the useState hook initializes the count variable with 0 and provides a setCount function to update it. Each time the button is clicked, the state changes, and the component re-renders with the updated value.

---

2. useEffect Hook

The **useEffect** hook is used to perform side effects in functional components. Side effects could include things like data fetching, subscriptions, or manually changing the DOM.

- It runs after the component renders.

- It can run on every render or only when specific state/props change.

Syntax:

```javascript
```

```javascript
useEffect(() => {
  // Code to run after component renders
}, [dependencies]);   // Array of dependencies (optional)
```

Example:

```javascript
```

```javascript
import React, { useState, useEffect } from 'react';
```

```
function Timer() {

  const [seconds, setSeconds] = useState(0);


  useEffect(() => {

    const interval = setInterval(() => {

      setSeconds(prevSeconds => prevSeconds +
1);

    }, 1000);


    // Cleanup function to clear the interval
when the component unmounts

    return () => clearInterval(interval);

  }, []);   // Empty dependency array means it
runs only once after the initial render


  return <p>Seconds: {seconds}</p>;

}


export default Timer;
```

In this example, the useEffect hook starts a timer that increments the seconds state every second. The empty dependency array [] ensures that the timer is set only once when the component mounts, and the cleanup function clears the interval when the component unmounts.

---

3. Custom Hooks

A **custom hook** is a function that uses React's built-in hooks to create reusable logic for your components. Custom hooks can be shared between components to keep your code DRY (Don't Repeat Yourself).

Example of a custom hook:

```javascript
import { useState, useEffect } from 'react';

function useLocalStorage(key, initialValue) {
  const [storedValue, setStoredValue] =
  useState(() => {
```

```
    try {

      const              item              =
window.localStorage.getItem(key);

        return   item   ?   JSON.parse(item)   :
initialValue;

      } catch (error) {

        return initialValue;

      }

    });


  const setValue = value => {

    try {

      setStoredValue(value);

      window.localStorage.setItem(key,
JSON.stringify(value));

      } catch (error) {

        console.error("Error      saving      to
localStorage", error);

      }

    };


  return [storedValue, setValue];
```

```
}
```

```
export default useLocalStorage;
```

In this custom hook, `useLocalStorage` manages the state of a value stored in the browser's `localStorage`. It initializes the state with the value in `localStorage` (if available) or falls back to `initialValue`. The hook also provides a function (`setValue`) to update the state and sync it with `localStorage`.

You can use it like this in a component:

```
javascript
```

```
import React from 'react';
import useLocalStorage from './useLocalStorage';

function App() {
  const        [name,        setName]        =
useLocalStorage('name', 'John Doe');
```

```
return (

  <div>

    <p>Name: {name}</p>

    <input

      type="text"

      value={name}

      onChange={(e)                          =>
setName(e.target.value)}   // Updates the value
and localStorage

      />

  </div>

  );

}



export default App;
```

Using Context API for State Management

React's **Context API** provides a way to share values like

state across your component tree without having to explicitly

pass props down through every level of the tree. This is

154

useful for global state management, such as user authentication, theming, or language settings.

To use the Context API, you need to:

1. **Create a Context** using `React.createContext()`.
2. **Provide a value** to the context at the top of your component tree.
3. **Consume the context value** inside components that need it.

1. Creating and Providing Context

```javascript
import React, { createContext, useState } from 'react';

// Create a Context
const CartContext = createContext();
```

```
// CartProvider component provides the cart
context value to its children
function CartProvider({ children }) {
  const [cart, setCart] = useState([]);

  const addToCart = (item) => {
    setCart([...cart, item]);
  };

  return (
    <CartContext.Provider      value={{      cart,
addToCart }}>
      {children}
    </CartContext.Provider>
  );
}


export { CartContext, CartProvider };
```

2. Consuming Context in a Component

```
javascript
```

```
import React, { useContext } from 'react';
import { CartContext } from './CartProvider';

function Cart() {
  const { cart } = useContext(CartContext);   // Access the cart from the context

  return (
    <div>
      <h2>Shopping Cart</h2>
      {cart.length === 0 ? (
        <p>Your cart is empty</p>
      ) : (
        <ul>
          {cart.map((item, index) => (
            <li key={index}>{item}</li>
          ))}
        </ul>
      )}
    </div>
  );
}
```

```javascript
export default Cart;
```

3. Using Context in App

```
javascript
```

```javascript
import React from 'react';
import { CartProvider } from './CartProvider';
import Cart from './Cart';


function App() {
  return (
    <CartProvider>
      <Cart />
    </CartProvider>
  );
}


export default App;
```

Example: Building a Dynamic Shopping Cart with React

Now, let's build a simple dynamic shopping cart using React, which will demonstrate the use of `useState`, `useEffect`, and the Context API.

Step 1: Setting Up the App

1. **Install React and Dependencies**: If you haven't already, create a new React app using `create-react-app` and install the necessary packages.

2. **Create Context for Cart**: In `CartProvider.js`, define the context to manage the cart's state.

```javascript
import React, { createContext, useState } from 'react';

const CartContext = createContext();

function CartProvider({ children }) {
  const [cart, setCart] = useState([]);
```

```
const addToCart = (item) => {

  setCart([...cart, item]);

};


return (

  <CartContext.Provider       value={{      cart,
addToCart }}>

    {children}

  </CartContext.Provider>

);

}


export { CartContext, CartProvider };
```

Step 2: Cart Component

In Cart.js, display the cart and allow items to be added.

javascript


```
import React, { useContext } from 'react';
import { CartContext } from './CartProvider';
```

```javascript
function Cart() {

  const { cart } = useContext(CartContext);


  return (

    <div>

      <h2>Shopping Cart</h2>

      {cart.length === 0 ? (

        <p>Your cart is empty</p>

      ) : (

        <ul>

          {cart.map((item, index) => (

            <li key={index}>{item}</li>

          ))}

        </ul>

      )}

    </div>

  );

}


export default Cart;
```

Step 3: Add Product Component

Create `AddProduct.js` to add products to the cart.

javascript

```
import React, { useContext } from 'react';
import { CartContext } from './CartProvider';


function AddProduct() {
  const { addToCart } = useContext(CartContext);


  const handleAddProduct = () => {
    addToCart('Product              '            +
Math.floor(Math.random() * 100));
  };


  return (
    <div>
      <button     onClick={handleAddProduct}>Add
Random Product</button>
    </div>
```

```
  );

}
```

```
export default AddProduct;
```

Step 4: App Component

In `App.js`, render the `AddProduct` and `Cart` components.

```javascript
import React from 'react';
import { CartProvider } from './CartProvider';
import Cart from './Cart';
import AddProduct from './AddProduct';

function App() {
  return (
    <CartProvider>
      <AddProduct />
      <Cart />
    </CartProvider>
  );
```

```
}
```

```
export default App;
```

Result:

- When you click the "Add Random Product" button, a product is added to the shopping cart, and the cart is displayed below with the list of added products.

Conclusion

In this chapter, we explored **React Hooks**, including useState and useEffect, which allow you to manage state and side effects in functional components. We also learned how to use **Context API** for state management, especially for sharing global state like a shopping cart. By combining these tools, you can build powerful, dynamic React applications like the shopping cart example, which can manage state and re-render efficiently based on user interaction.

CHAPTER 13

BACKEND DEVELOPMENT:

INTRODUCTION TO NODE.JS

What is Node.js and Why It's Popular for Backend Development

Node.js is an open-source, cross-platform runtime environment that allows developers to execute JavaScript code on the server-side. Traditionally, JavaScript was used exclusively for client-side development in web browsers, but with the introduction of Node.js, JavaScript can now be used to build server-side applications as well.

Key features that make Node.js popular for backend development:

1. **Non-blocking, Asynchronous I/O**: Node.js uses non-blocking, event-driven architecture, which makes it efficient for handling I/O operations (such as reading from databases, handling HTTP requests, etc.) without waiting for operations to complete before moving on to the next task. This makes Node.js ideal for building scalable and high-performance applications.

2. **Single Programming Language**: With Node.js, developers can use JavaScript for both frontend (client-side) and backend (server-side) development, which streamlines the development process and eliminates the need for context switching between different programming languages.

3. **Fast and Lightweight**: Node.js is built on Google Chrome's V8 JavaScript engine, which compiles JavaScript into native machine code for fast execution. It's well-suited for building fast and

lightweight applications, especially real-time web apps.

4. **Large Ecosystem**: Node.js has a vast ecosystem of modules available via the **npm** (Node Package Manager), making it easy to add features to your application without reinventing the wheel.

5. **Scalable**: Node.js is designed to handle many simultaneous connections with minimal overhead, making it an excellent choice for building scalable, real-time applications like chat apps, live data feeds, or gaming platforms.

Setting Up a Basic Server with Node.js

To get started with Node.js, you'll need to install it on your machine. You can download Node.js from its official website: https://nodejs.org/.

Once installed, you can verify the installation by running the following commands in your terminal or command prompt:

```bash
node -v   # Check Node.js version
npm -v    # Check npm version
```

Setting Up a Basic HTTP Server

Let's build a simple HTTP server with Node.js using the built-in **http** module.

1. **Create a new directory** for your project and navigate into it:

   ```bash
   mkdir node-server
   cd node-server
   ```

2. **Create a file named `server.js`** and add the following code to set up a basic HTTP server:

169

```javascript
const http = require('http');   // Import
the built-in http module

const server = http.createServer((req,
res) => {
    res.statusCode = 200;   // Set the
status code to 200 (OK)
    res.setHeader('Content-Type',
'text/plain');
    res.end('Hello, World!\n');   // Send a
response to the client
});

const PORT = 3000;
server.listen(PORT, () => {
    console.log(`Server is running on
http://localhost:${PORT}`);
});
```

3. **Run the server** by executing the following command in your terminal:

```bash
```

```
node server.js
```

4. Open a browser and navigate to http://localhost:3000. You should see the message: "Hello, World!"

Example: Building a Simple API with Express

While Node.js is great for creating simple HTTP servers, most backend applications use **Express.js**, a popular web framework that simplifies building APIs and web applications.

Step 1: Install Express

1. In your project directory, run the following command to install Express:

```bash
npm init -y  // Initializes a new Node.js
project and generates a package.json file
npm install express   // Installs the
Express framework
```

Step 2: Create a Basic Express Server

1. Create a file called `app.js` and add the following code to set up a basic Express server:

```javascript
const express = require('express');   //
Import the Express module
const app = express();   // Create an
Express app

// Middleware to handle JSON requests
```

```javascript
app.use(express.json());


// Define a simple route to return a "Hello World" message
app.get('/', (req, res) => {
    res.send('Hello World!');
});


// Define a simple API endpoint that returns JSON data
app.get('/api/greet', (req, res) => {
    const greeting = { message: 'Hello from the API!' };
    res.json(greeting);   // Send a JSON response
});


// Start the server on port 3000
const PORT = 3000;
app.listen(PORT, () => {
    console.log(`Server is running on http://localhost:${PORT}`);
```

```
});
```

Step 3: Run the Server

1. In the terminal, run the following command to start the server:

```bash
bash
```

```
node app.js
```

2. Open a browser and navigate to http://localhost:3000. You should see the message: "Hello World!"

3. Now, visit http://localhost:3000/api/greet. You should receive the following JSON response:

```json
json
```

```
{ "message": "Hello from the API!" }
```

Step 4: Handling HTTP Methods

You can define different routes for various HTTP methods such as GET, POST, PUT, and DELETE. Here's an example of a POST endpoint to handle incoming data:

javascript

```javascript
// POST route to receive data from a client
app.post('/api/greet', (req, res) => {
    const { name } = req.body;   // Extract name
from the request body
    const greetingMessage = `Hello, ${name}!`;
    res.json({ message: greetingMessage });   //
Send a personalized greeting as a JSON response
});
```

- This POST endpoint accepts JSON data and returns a personalized message.

To test this, you can use **Postman** or **Insomnia** to send a POST request to http://localhost:3000/api/greet with the following body:

```
json
```

```json
{
    "name": "Alice"
}
```

The response will be:

```
json
```

```json
{
    "message": "Hello, Alice!"
}
```

Step 5: Adding More Routes

You can define additional routes for more functionality. For example:

```
javascript
```

```javascript
// A route to return a list of users (GET request)
app.get('/api/users', (req, res) => {
```

```
const users = [
    { id: 1, name: 'Alice' },
    { id: 2, name: 'Bob' }
];
res.json(users);  // Send the list of users as
a JSON response
});
```

Conclusion

In this chapter, we covered the basics of **Node.js** and how it enables you to build fast, scalable web applications using JavaScript on the server-side. We also introduced **Express.js**, a popular web framework that simplifies the creation of APIs and web servers.

With Express, you can easily define routes, handle HTTP methods (GET, POST, etc.), and manage middleware to handle requests and responses. We also saw how to build a simple API that handles GET and POST requests and returns JSON data.

By mastering Node.js and Express, you can build robust and efficient backend services for your web applications, handling everything from simple APIs to complex server-side logic.

CHAPTER 14

DATABASES: WORKING WITH SQL AND NOSQL DATABASES

Introduction to SQL vs NoSQL Databases

When building web applications, you will often need to store and retrieve data. The two main types of databases you'll encounter are **SQL** (Structured Query Language) and **NoSQL** (Not Only SQL) databases. Each type of database has its own characteristics, and knowing when to use each is important for your application's performance, scalability, and data structure.

1. SQL Databases (Relational Databases)

- **SQL databases** store data in structured tables with rows and columns. These databases are known as **relational**

databases because they organize data into relationships (e.g., foreign keys).

- **Schema**: SQL databases have a predefined schema that defines the structure of the data, meaning each table has a specific structure that does not change easily.

- **ACID properties**: SQL databases follow ACID (Atomicity, Consistency, Isolation, Durability) properties to ensure that transactions are processed reliably.

Examples of SQL databases:

- MySQL
- PostgreSQL
- SQLite
- Microsoft SQL Server

SQL Query Example:

```sql
SELECT * FROM users WHERE id = 1;
```

2. NoSQL Databases (Non-Relational Databases)

- **NoSQL databases** are designed for more flexible data storage. Instead of tables with rows and columns, NoSQL databases often store data in formats like documents, key-value pairs, graphs, or wide-column stores.

- **Schema-less**: NoSQL databases are more flexible with the schema, meaning they can handle semi-structured or unstructured data.

- **Eventual Consistency**: Unlike SQL databases, NoSQL databases often prioritize performance and scalability over strict ACID compliance, and they tend to be more suitable for distributed applications.

Examples of NoSQL databases:

- MongoDB (Document-based)
- Cassandra (Wide-column)
- Redis (Key-value store)
- Neo4j (Graph database)

NoSQL Query Example (MongoDB):

```
javascript


db.users.find({ id: 1 });
```

Using MongoDB and MySQL with JavaScript

1. Using MongoDB with JavaScript

MongoDB is a popular NoSQL database that stores data in a flexible, JSON-like format called BSON (Binary JSON). MongoDB allows you to work with collections of documents, where each document can have a different structure.

To interact with MongoDB from JavaScript, you can use the official **MongoDB Node.js driver** or **Mongoose**, a popular ODM (Object Data Modeling) library that simplifies working with MongoDB.

Setting Up MongoDB:

1. **Install MongoDB**: First, install MongoDB locally or use a cloud service like **MongoDB Atlas**.

2. **Install the MongoDB Node.js Driver**:

```bash
npm install mongoose
```

Basic Example of Using MongoDB in Node.js:

```javascript
const mongoose = require('mongoose');

mongoose.connect('mongodb://localhost/mydatabase', { useNewUrlParser: true, useUnifiedTopology: true })
  .then(() => console.log('MongoDB connected'))
  .catch((err) => console.error('MongoDB connection error:', err));

// Define a schema for a blog post
const postSchema = new mongoose.Schema({
```

183

```javascript
  title: String,

  content: String,

  author: String,

  date: { type: Date, default: Date.now }
});


// Create a model based on the schema
const Post = mongoose.model('Post', postSchema);


// Create a new blog post
const newPost = new Post({
  title: 'My First Post',
  content: 'This is the content of my first
post.',
  author: 'Alice'
});


// Save the new post to MongoDB
newPost.save()
  .then(() => console.log('Post saved'))
  .catch((err) => console.error('Error saving
post:', err));
```

2. Using MySQL with JavaScript

MySQL is a popular relational database management system (RDBMS) that uses SQL to manage data in structured tables.

To interact with MySQL from JavaScript, you can use the **mysql2** or **sequelize** library for Node.js.

Setting Up MySQL:

1. **Install MySQL**: Download and install MySQL locally, or use a cloud MySQL service.

2. **Install the MySQL2 Node.js Library**:

```bash
bash
```

```bash
npm install mysql2
```

Basic Example of Using MySQL in Node.js:

```javascript
javascript
```

```javascript
const mysql = require('mysql2');


// Create a connection to the MySQL database
const connection = mysql.createConnection({
  host: 'localhost',
  user: 'root',   // Use your MySQL username
  password: '',   // Use your MySQL password
  database: 'mydatabase'
});


// Connect to the database
connection.connect((err) => {
  if (err) throw err;
  console.log('Connected to MySQL');
});


// Query the database
connection.query('SELECT * FROM posts', (err,
results) => {
  if (err) throw err;
  console.log(results);
});
```

```
// Insert data into the database
const post = { title: 'My First Post', content:
'This is the content of my first post.' };
connection.query('INSERT INTO posts SET ?', post,
(err, res) => {
  if (err) throw err;
  console.log('Post inserted:', res.insertId);
});


// Close the connection
connection.end();
```

Example: Building a Blog App with MongoDB and Node.js

Now let's build a simple blog app using **MongoDB** and **Node.js** with the **Express** framework. This app will allow users to create and view blog posts.

187

Step 1: Setting Up the Project

1. **Create a new Node.js project**:

   bash

   ```bash
   mkdir blog-app
   cd blog-app
   npm init -y
   npm install express mongoose body-parser
   ```

2. **Create a basic server with Express**: Create a file called `app.js` and set up the server:

   javascript

   ```javascript
   const express = require('express');
   const mongoose = require('mongoose');
   const bodyParser = require('body-parser');

   const app = express();
   const PORT = 3000;
   ```

```
// Connect to MongoDB
mongoose.connect('mongodb://localhost/blo
g',        {        useNewUrlParser:        true,
useUnifiedTopology: true })
   .then(()        =>        console.log('MongoDB
connected'))
   .catch((err)    =>    console.log('MongoDB
connection error:', err));


app.use(bodyParser.json());


// Define a Schema for the blog post
const postSchema = new mongoose.Schema({
   title: String,
   content: String,
   author: String,
   date: { type: Date, default: Date.now }
});


const    Post    =    mongoose.model('Post',
postSchema);
```

```javascript
// Route to get all posts
app.get('/posts', (req, res) => {
  Post.find()
    .then(posts => res.json(posts))
    .catch(err => res.status(500).json({
error: err }));
});


// Route to create a new post
app.post('/posts', (req, res) => {
  const newPost = new Post(req.body);
  newPost.save()
    .then(post => res.json(post))
    .catch(err => res.status(500).json({
error: err }));
});


app.listen(PORT, () => {
  console.log(`Server is running on
http://localhost:${PORT}`);
});
```

Step 2: Running the Server

1. **Run the server**:

   bash

   ```
   node app.js
   ```

2. Open your browser and visit http://localhost:3000/posts. You will see an empty array of posts initially.

3. Use **Postman** or **Insomnia** to send a POST request to `http://localhost:3000/posts` with the following JSON data to create a new post:

   json

   ```
   {
     "title": "My First Blog Post",
     "content": "This is the content of my first post.",
     "author": "Alice"
   ```

```
}
```

4. After successfully posting, visit http://localhost:3000/posts again, and you should see the newly created blog post.

Conclusion

In this chapter, we explored both **SQL** (MySQL) and **NoSQL** (MongoDB) databases, understanding their differences and use cases. We also learned how to interact with MongoDB and MySQL from JavaScript and built a simple **blog application** using **MongoDB** and **Node.js**.

- **MongoDB** is well-suited for applications with flexible, schema-less data structures.
- **MySQL** is ideal for structured data with relationships that need to be managed using SQL.

By combining **Express**, **MongoDB**, and **Node.js**, we can easily build scalable and dynamic applications that interact with databases to store and manage data efficiently.

CHAPTER 15

BUILDING RESTFUL APIS WITH NODE.JS AND EXPRESS

Understanding REST and HTTP Methods

A **RESTful API** (Representational State Transfer) is an architectural style for building web services that are lightweight, stateless, and designed to operate over HTTP. REST is based on the concept of resources (e.g., users, posts, books) and uses standard HTTP methods to interact with those resources.

Key concepts of REST:

1. **Resources**: Entities in your application that can be accessed via URLs (e.g., /users, /posts, /books).

2. **Stateless**: Each request from a client must contain all the information the server needs to process the request, and

194

the server does not store any session information about the client.

3. **HTTP Methods**:

- o **GET**: Retrieve data from the server (e.g., get a list of books or a specific book).

- o **POST**: Create new data on the server (e.g., add a new book).

- o **PUT**: Update existing data on the server (e.g., update the details of a book).

- o **DELETE**: Delete data on the server (e.g., remove a book from the inventory).

Each of these methods is mapped to a specific CRUD (Create, Read, Update, Delete) operation:

- **GET** → Read
- **POST** → Create
- **PUT** → Update
- **DELETE** → Delete

Building a RESTful API with Node.js and Express

We'll use **Express**, a minimal web framework for Node.js, to build our RESTful API. Express simplifies the creation of routes, handling HTTP requests, and managing middleware.

Step 1: Setting Up the Project

1. **Initialize a New Node.js Project**: Create a new directory for the project, initialize a new Node.js project, and install the necessary dependencies.

```bash
mkdir bookstore-api
cd bookstore-api
npm init -y
npm install express body-parser
```

2. **Create app.js**: Create a file called app.js and set up the basic server with Express.

Step 2: Building the API

Now, let's build a simple API for a book store with basic CRUD operations.

app.js:

javascript

```javascript
const express = require('express');
const bodyParser = require('body-parser');

const app = express();
const PORT = 3000;

// Middleware to parse JSON bodies
app.use(bodyParser.json());

// Sample book data (to simulate a database)
let books = [
  { id: 1, title: '1984', author: 'George Orwell', year: 1949 },
```

```javascript
  { id: 2, title: 'To Kill a Mockingbird',
author: 'Harper Lee', year: 1960 }
];


// GET: Retrieve all books
app.get('/api/books', (req, res) => {
  res.json(books);  // Respond with all books
});


// GET: Retrieve a single book by id
app.get('/api/books/:id', (req, res) => {
  const bookId = parseInt(req.params.id);
  const book = books.find(b => b.id === bookId);
  if (book) {
    res.json(book);
  } else {
    res.status(404).send('Book not found');
  }
});


// POST: Create a new book
app.post('/api/books', (req, res) => {
```

```
const newBook = req.body;
if (!newBook.title || !newBook.author ||
!newBook.year) {
    return res.status(400).send('Missing
required fields');
}


newBook.id = books.length + 1;  // Assign a new
ID
books.push(newBook);  // Add the new book to
the array
res.status(201).json(newBook);  // Return the
newly created book
});


// PUT: Update an existing book by id
app.put('/api/books/:id', (req, res) => {
const bookId = parseInt(req.params.id);
const updatedData = req.body;


let book = books.find(b => b.id === bookId);
if (!book) {
```

```
    return      res.status(404).send('Book      not
found');

  }


  // Update book details
  book = { ...book, ...updatedData };
  books = books.map(b => (b.id === bookId ? book
: b));
  res.json(book);
});


// DELETE: Delete a book by id
app.delete('/api/books/:id', (req, res) => {
  const bookId = parseInt(req.params.id);
  const bookIndex = books.findIndex(b => b.id ===
bookId);


  if (bookIndex === -1) {
    return      res.status(404).send('Book      not
found');

  }
```

```
  books.splice(bookIndex, 1);  // Remove the book
from the array
  res.status(204).send();    // Respond with no
content (204)
});
```

```
// Start the server
app.listen(PORT, () => {
  console.log(`Server      is      running      on
http://localhost:${PORT}`);
});
```

Step 3: Testing the API

Once the server is running, you can test the different routes

using **Postman**, **Insomnia**, or **cURL**.

1. **GET** /api/books:

   o Retrieves the list of all books.

   o **Response**: A JSON array of books.

2. **GET** /api/books/:id:

   o Retrieves a specific book by ID.

- o Example: GET

  `http://localhost:3000/api/books/1.`

- o **Response**: A JSON object for the specified book.

3. **POST** `/api/books`:

   - o Adds a new book to the store.

   - o Example: Send the following JSON in the request body:

     `json`

     ```
     {

       "title": "The Great Gatsby",

       "author": "F. Scott Fitzgerald",

       "year": 1925

     }
     ```

   - o **Response**: The newly created book with an assigned `id`.

4. **PUT** `/api/books/:id`:

   - o Updates an existing book by ID.

o Example: PUT

`http://localhost:3000/api/books/1`

with the following JSON in the request body:

`json`

```
{

  "title": "1984 (Updated Edition)",

  "author": "George Orwell",

  "year": 1950

}
```

o **Response**: The updated book with the new data.

5. **DELETE** `/api/books/:id`:

o Deletes a book by ID.

o Example: DELETE

`http://localhost:3000/api/books/2`.

o **Response**: Status code `204` for a successful deletion.

Step 4: Conclusion and Further Enhancements

In this chapter, we built a basic **RESTful API** using **Node.js** and **Express** to manage a book store. The API supports the standard CRUD operations:

- **GET** to retrieve data,
- **POST** to create new data,
- **PUT** to update existing data,
- **DELETE** to remove data.

You can extend this application by adding features like:

1. **Validation**: Add more advanced input validation (e.g., using a library like **Joi**).
2. **Persistent Storage**: Connect the API to a database like **MongoDB** or **MySQL** instead of using in-memory data.
3. **Authentication**: Implement JWT (JSON Web Token) authentication for secure access to certain routes.

By following REST principles and using HTTP methods appropriately, this API provides a solid foundation for building scalable web services.

CHAPTER 16

AUTHENTICATION AND AUTHORIZATION: SECURING YOUR APPLICATIONS

Understanding Authentication and Authorization

In web applications, **authentication** and **authorization** are two fundamental concepts that ensure the security and integrity of user data and application logic.

1. **Authentication**:

   o Authentication is the process of verifying the identity of a user. It confirms that the user is who they claim to be.

   o This typically involves providing a set of credentials (like a username and password), and the server checks whether those credentials are valid.

2. **Authorization**:

o   Authorization, on the other hand, determines what an authenticated user is allowed to do or access in the system. Once the system has verified who the user is, authorization controls their permissions, such as access to certain pages, resources, or actions.

o   For example, an admin might have permission to create or delete content, while a regular user may only be able to view content.

Together, **authentication** and **authorization** are used to ensure that only the right users can access certain resources in your application, and that they only have access to the appropriate data and functionality.

Using JWT (JSON Web Tokens) and Passport.js for User Authentication

JWT (JSON Web Tokens)

JSON Web Tokens (JWT) are a compact, URL-safe means of representing claims between two parties. They are commonly used for **user authentication** in modern web applications, especially in single-page applications (SPAs) and APIs.

A JWT is composed of three parts:

1. **Header**: Contains the type of token (JWT) and the signing algorithm used (e.g., HMAC SHA256 or RSA).

2. **Payload**: Contains the claims (user information, roles, permissions, etc.). This is the part that is used for authentication and authorization.

3. **Signature**: A cryptographic signature to verify that the token was not tampered with. It is created using the header, payload, and a secret key.

JWTs are typically used in **stateless authentication**, meaning the server does not store session information. Instead, the client sends the token with each request, and the server verifies it.

Passport.js

Passport.js is a popular authentication middleware for Node.js. It provides a simple and consistent API for handling various types of authentication strategies, including username/password, OAuth, and JWT.

Passport.js is flexible and can be used with **JWT** to authenticate users using tokens, making it ideal for modern web applications.

Example: Building a Secure Login System with JWT and Passport.js

In this example, we'll build a secure login system with **Node.js**, **Express**, **Passport.js**, and **JWT**. We'll create:

- A simple **user authentication** system.
- Use **JWT** for token-based authentication.
- Use **Passport.js** to manage user login and authentication.

Step 1: Set Up the Project

1. **Initialize the Node.js Project**:

   ```bash
   mkdir secure-login
   cd secure-login
   npm init -y
   npm install express mongoose passport passport-local jsonwebtoken bcryptjs body-parser
   ```

2. **Create the Directory Structure**:

   o   server.js - Main server file.

- o models/User.js - User model for storing user data.

- o config/passport.js - Passport configuration file.

- o routes/auth.js - Authentication routes.

Step 2: Set Up the User Model

We will create a User model to store user information such as username, email, and password.

models/User.js:

javascript

```
const mongoose = require('mongoose');
const bcrypt = require('bcryptjs');


const userSchema = new mongoose.Schema({
  username: { type: String, required: true,
unique: true },
  password: { type: String, required: true },
```

```
});


// Encrypt password before saving to the database
userSchema.pre('save', async function (next) {
    if    (!this.isModified('password'))    return
next();
    this.password              =              await
bcrypt.hash(this.password, 10);
    next();
});


// Compare password
userSchema.methods.comparePassword  =  function
(candidatePassword) {
    return        bcrypt.compare(candidatePassword,
this.password);
};


module.exports    =    mongoose.model('User',
userSchema);
```

Step 3: Set Up Passport.js for Local Authentication

Passport.js will use the **Local Strategy** to authenticate users using their username and password.

config/passport.js:

javascript

```
const passport = require('passport');
const LocalStrategy = require('passport-
local').Strategy;
const User = require('../models/User');

// Configure Passport to use Local Strategy
passport.use(new LocalStrategy({
  usernameField: 'username',
  passwordField: 'password',
}, async (username, password, done) => {
  try {
    const user = await User.findOne({ username
});
```

```
    if (!user) return done(null, false, {
message: 'User not found' });


    const     isMatch     =     await
user.comparePassword(password);
    if (!isMatch) return done(null, false, {
message: 'Incorrect password' });


    return done(null, user);
  } catch (err) {
    return done(err);

  }
}));


passport.serializeUser((user, done) => {
  done(null, user.id);  // Serialize user ID into
the session
});


passport.deserializeUser(async (id, done) => {
  try {
    const user = await User.findById(id);
```

```javascript
    done(null, user);   // Deserialize user from
the session using the ID
  } catch (err) {
    done(err);

  }
});
```

Step 4: Set Up JWT Authentication

We'll generate a JWT token upon successful login and send it to the client. The client can then use the token for subsequent requests.

routes/auth.js:

javascript

```javascript
const express = require('express');
const jwt = require('jsonwebtoken');
const passport = require('passport');
const User = require('../models/User');
const router = express.Router();
```

```javascript
// JWT Secret Key

const JWT_SECRET = 'your-secret-key';


// Register Route

router.post('/register', async (req, res) => {

  const { username, password } = req.body;

  try {

    const user = new User({ username, password
});

    await user.save();

    res.status(201).json({    message:    'User
registered' });

  } catch (err) {

    res.status(400).json({    message:    'Error
registering user' });

  }

});


// Login Route

router.post('/login',

passport.authenticate('local', { session: false
}), (req, res) => {
```

```javascript
// Generate JWT token after successful login
const payload = { id: req.user.id, username: req.user.username };
const token = jwt.sign(payload, JWT_SECRET, { expiresIn: '1h' });
res.json({ token });
});


// Protected Route Example
router.get('/protected', (req, res) => {
const token = req.headers.authorization?.split(' ')[1]; // Bearer token from headers
if (!token) return res.status(401).json({ message: 'Unauthorized' });


jwt.verify(token, JWT_SECRET, (err, decoded) => {
if (err) return res.status(401).json({ message: 'Invalid token' });
res.json({ message: 'Protected data', user: decoded });
```

```
  });

});
```

```
module.exports = router;
```

Step 5: Set Up the Server

Finally, we'll create the `server.js` file, which will initialize the Express app, set up Passport.js, and start the server.

server.js:

javascript

```
const express = require('express');
const mongoose = require('mongoose');
const passport = require('passport');
const bodyParser = require('body-parser');
const authRoutes = require('./routes/auth');
require('./config/passport');    //   Initialize
passport configuration

const app = express();
```

```javascript
const PORT = 3000;

// Middleware
app.use(bodyParser.json());
app.use(passport.initialize());

// MongoDB connection
mongoose.connect('mongodb://localhost/auth-demo', { useNewUrlParser: true, useUnifiedTopology: true })
  .then(() => console.log('MongoDB connected'))
  .catch((err) => console.log('MongoDB connection error:', err));

// Routes
app.use('/api/auth', authRoutes);

// Start the server
app.listen(PORT, () => {
  console.log(`Server running on http://localhost:${PORT}`);
});
```

Step 6: Testing the API

1. **Register a User**: Use Postman to send a POST request to `http://localhost:3000/api/auth/register` with the following JSON body:

```json
json

{

  "username": "john_doe",
  "password": "password123"

}
```

2. **Login**: Send a POST request to `http://localhost:3000/api/auth/login` with the same credentials (username and password). The response will contain a JWT token.

3. **Access Protected Route**: Send a GET request to `http://localhost:3000/api/auth/protected` with the **Authorization** header:

```makefile
makefile
```

220

```
Authorization: Bearer <JWT_TOKEN>
```

4. If the token is valid, you will get access to protected data; otherwise, you'll receive an "Unauthorized" error.

Conclusion

In this chapter, we learned about **authentication** and **authorization** and how to secure our applications using **JWT** for token-based authentication. We also explored how to integrate **Passport.js** for handling user login and built a simple secure login system using **Node.js** and **Express**.

By using **JWT**, we can implement a stateless authentication mechanism where the server does not store session information, and the client sends the token for each request.

This system is widely used in modern web applications, particularly for single-page apps (SPAs) and APIs.

Chapter 17: Full-Stack Development with JavaScript: Connecting the Frontend and Backend

Integrating the Frontend and Backend with JavaScript

In a full-stack application, the **frontend** (client-side) is responsible for the user interface and user experience, while the **backend** (server-side) handles data processing, business logic, and communication with the database. The frontend and backend need to communicate with each other to exchange data and enable dynamic behavior within the application.

JavaScript can be used on both the **frontend** and **backend**:

- **Frontend**: JavaScript is typically used with frameworks/libraries like **React**, **Vue**, or **Angular** to build interactive UIs.

- **Backend**: JavaScript, using **Node.js**, is used to build APIs and handle server-side logic.

The key to integrating the frontend and backend is to ensure they can communicate seamlessly via HTTP requests. This communication can be done using:

- **AJAX (Asynchronous JavaScript and XML)**: A technique that allows sending and receiving data asynchronously without reloading the web page.
- **Fetch API**: A modern alternative to AJAX for making network requests. It provides a cleaner syntax and works with promises.

Using AJAX and Fetch API to Connect to the Backend

1. AJAX (Asynchronous JavaScript and XML)

AJAX allows us to send HTTP requests asynchronously to a backend server, process the response, and update the web page dynamically without refreshing the page. It was traditionally used with the XMLHttpRequest object, but with modern JavaScript, **the Fetch API** is preferred.

Example of a basic AJAX request using XMLHttpRequest:

javascript

```javascript
const xhr = new XMLHttpRequest();
xhr.open('GET',
'http://localhost:3000/api/posts', true);
xhr.onload = function () {
   if (xhr.status === 200) {
     const posts = JSON.parse(xhr.responseText);
     console.log(posts);   // Handle the response
here
   }
};
xhr.send();
```

225

This method is a bit cumbersome and can lead to "callback hell" when dealing with multiple asynchronous operations. That's why **Fetch API** is commonly used in modern JavaScript applications.

---

2. Fetch API

The **Fetch API** provides a simpler way to make HTTP requests and returns **Promises**. It supports all modern browsers and offers a more flexible approach to making asynchronous network requests.

Example of using the Fetch API to get data from the backend:

javascript

```
fetch('http://localhost:3000/api/posts')
  .then(response => response.json())   // Parse
the JSON data from the response
  .then(posts => {
```

```
    console.log(posts);  // Handle the fetched
data here
  })
  .catch(error => {
    console.error('Error    fetching    posts:',
error);
  });
```

The **Fetch API** is promise-based, making it easier to work with than the old XMLHttpRequest object.

Example of using POST with Fetch API:

javascript

```
const newPost = {
  title: "My New Post",
  content: "This is the content of my new post"
};


fetch('http://localhost:3000/api/posts', {
  method: 'POST',
  headers: {
```

```
    'Content-Type': 'application/json',
  },
  body: JSON.stringify(newPost),
})
  .then(response => response.json())
  .then(data => {
    console.log('New post created:', data);
  })
  .catch(error => {
    console.error('Error    creating    post:',
error);
  });
```

This POST request sends new post data to the backend, where it can be processed and saved in the database.

Example: Building a Full-Stack Social Media App

Let's create a simple **full-stack social media app** where users can post content. We'll build the **frontend** using

HTML, CSS, and **JavaScript** (with Fetch API), and the **backend** using **Node.js**, **Express**, and **MongoDB**.

Step 1: Backend Setup with Node.js, Express, and MongoDB

1. **Install dependencies**:

bash

```
mkdir social-media-app
cd social-media-app
npm init -y
npm install express mongoose body-parser cors
```

2. **Create the backend server**: Create a file called `server.js` to set up the server with **Express** and **MongoDB**.

server.js:

javascript

```
const express = require('express');
```

```javascript
const mongoose = require('mongoose');
const bodyParser = require('body-parser');
const cors = require('cors');

// Initialize the app
const app = express();
const PORT = 3000;

// Middleware
app.use(cors());   // Enable CORS for frontend-
backend communication
app.use(bodyParser.json());      // Parse JSON
request bodies

// MongoDB connection
mongoose.connect('mongodb://localhost/social-
media',      {      useNewUrlParser:      true,
useUnifiedTopology: true })
  .then(() => console.log('MongoDB connected'))
  .catch(err => console.log('MongoDB connection
error:', err));
```

```javascript
// Define a schema for posts
const postSchema = new mongoose.Schema({
  title: String,
  content: String,
  date: { type: Date, default: Date.now }
});


// Create a model based on the schema
const Post = mongoose.model('Post', postSchema);


// Routes
app.get('/api/posts', async (req, res) => {
  try {
    const posts = await Post.find();
    res.json(posts);
  } catch (err) {
    res.status(500).send('Error        retrieving
posts');
  }
});


app.post('/api/posts', async (req, res) => {
```

```
const newPost = new Post(req.body);

try {

  const savedPost = await newPost.save();

  res.status(201).json(savedPost);

} catch (err) {

  res.status(500).send('Error saving post');

  }

});


// Start the server

app.listen(PORT, () => {

  console.log(`Server          running          on

http://localhost:${PORT}`);

});
```

- The /api/posts **GET** route fetches all posts from MongoDB.

- The /api/posts **POST** route creates a new post and saves it to the database.

Step 2: Frontend Setup with HTML, CSS, and JavaScript

1. **Create the frontend**: Create a basic HTML page with a form to submit posts and display the list of posts.

index.html:

```
html
```

```
<!DOCTYPE html>
<html lang="en">
<head>
  <meta charset="UTF-8">
  <meta name="viewport" content="width=device-width, initial-scale=1.0">
  <title>Social Media App</title>
  <style>
    body { font-family: Arial, sans-serif; }
    .post { border: 1px solid #ccc; padding: 10px; margin-bottom: 10px; }
  </style>
</head>
<body>
```

```html
<h1>Social Media App</h1>


<h2>Create a New Post</h2>
<form id="postForm">
    <input          type="text"          id="title"
placeholder="Title" required />
    <textarea id="content" placeholder="Content"
required></textarea>
    <button type="submit">Submit Post</button>
</form>


<h2>Posts</h2>
<div id="postsList"></div>


<script>
    // Fetch posts and display them
    function fetchPosts() {
      fetch('http://localhost:3000/api/posts')
        .then(response => response.json())
        .then(posts => {
          const          postsList          =
document.getElementById('postsList');
```

```javascript
        postsList.innerHTML = '';

        posts.forEach(post => {

            const        postDiv        =
document.createElement('div');

            postDiv.className = 'post';

            postDiv.innerHTML                =
`<h3>${post.title}</h3><p>${post.content}</p><s
mall>${new
Date(post.date).toLocaleString()}</small>`;

            postsList.appendChild(postDiv);

        });

      })

      .catch(err    =>    console.error('Error
fetching posts:', err));

    }


    // Handle form submission to create a new
post

document.getElementById('postForm').addEventLis
tener('submit', function (e) {

        e.preventDefault();
```

```
const newPost = {

  title:
document.getElementById('title').value,

  content:
document.getElementById('content').value

  };


fetch('http://localhost:3000/api/posts', {

  method: 'POST',

  headers:           {           'Content-Type':
'application/json' },

  body: JSON.stringify(newPost)

})

  .then(response => response.json())

  .then(post => {

    console.log('Post created:', post);

    fetchPosts();  // Reload the posts list

  })

  .catch(err    =>    console.error('Error
creating post:', err));

});
```

```
// Initial fetch of posts

fetchPosts();

  </script>

</body>

</html>
```

Step 3: Running the Application

1. **Start the backend server**: Run the backend server by executing:

```bash
bash
```

```
node server.js
```

2. **Open the frontend**: Open the `index.html` file in a web browser.

- **Create a post**: Enter a title and content, then click "Submit Post." The post will be saved to MongoDB.
- **View the posts**: The list of posts will be displayed on the page.

Conclusion

In this chapter, we explored how to build a **full-stack social media app** using **JavaScript** for both the frontend and backend. We used **Node.js** and **Express** for the backend, with **MongoDB** to store data, and **Fetch API** to handle communication between the frontend and backend.

Key concepts covered:

- **Connecting frontend and backend** with **AJAX** and **Fetch API**.
- **Building a full-stack application** where users can create and view posts.
- **Handling GET and POST requests** to interact with data.

With these skills, you can start building more complex applications and connect your frontend and backend seamlessly using JavaScript.

CHAPTER 18

DEPLOYING YOUR APPLICATION AND BEST PRACTICES

Introduction to Deployment and Hosting Services

When your application is ready to be shared with users, the next step is **deployment**—putting your application on a server so that people can access it. Deployment also includes setting up hosting services, managing databases, configuring environment variables, and handling continuous integration/continuous deployment (CI/CD).

There are various hosting and deployment platforms available, depending on the type of application you are building.

Hosting Platforms for Full-Stack Applications:

1. **Heroku**: A cloud platform that simplifies the deployment of web applications, supporting multiple programming languages including Node.js. It's a great platform for deploying full-stack apps with minimal configuration.

2. **Netlify**: Ideal for static websites or frontend-only applications, but it can also handle full-stack apps using serverless functions. It offers a seamless integration with GitHub for automatic deployments.

3. **Vercel**: A popular choice for frontend frameworks (like React, Next.js), it also supports backend services with serverless functions.

4. **AWS (Amazon Web Services)** and **Google Cloud Platform (GCP)**: Provide more control and customization but require more configuration. These services offer full-stack hosting, database integration, and storage solutions.

Best Practices for Code Structure, Version Control (Git), and Testing

When developing an application, especially one that will be deployed and maintained over time, there are several **best practices** that can help you maintain code quality, collaboration, and reliability.

1. Code Structure

A clear and logical project structure makes your codebase easier to maintain, scale, and collaborate on. Here's a common structure for a full-stack app:

bash

```
/my-app
  /client (Frontend)
    /src
      /components
```

242

```
    /assets

    /styles

  package.json

  index.html

/server (Backend)

  /controllers

  /models

  /routes

  server.js

/config

  database.js

.gitignore

package.json

README.md
```

- **Frontend**: Contains the React (or other frameworks) code in the /client directory, including components, assets (like images), and styles.

- **Backend**: Contains server-side logic like routes, controllers, and models inside the /server directory.

- **Config**: Centralized configuration files for environment variables or database connection setups.

243

2. Version Control with Git

Version control is critical for managing code changes and collaborating with others. **Git** is the most widely used version control system.

- **Initialize Git**:

  bash

  ```
  git init    # Initializes a new Git
  repository
  ```

- **Add files and commit**:

  bash

  ```
  git add .  # Stages all files for commit
  git commit -m "Initial commit"  # Commits
  the changes
  ```

- **Using GitHub/GitLab**:

o Push code to a remote repository for backup and collaboration:

```
bash
```

```
git        remote      add       origin
https://github.com/your-
username/your-repo.git
git push -u origin master
```

- **Branching**: When working in teams, create branches for new features or bug fixes.

```
bash
```

```
git checkout -b new-feature  # Create and
switch to a new branch
git merge new-feature  # Merge the branch
back into the master branch
```

3. Testing

Testing is essential for ensuring that your application works as expected and for preventing bugs. Common types of tests include:

- **Unit Tests**: Test individual functions or components.

- **Integration Tests**: Test how different parts of the application work together.

- **End-to-End (E2E) Tests**: Test the entire flow of the application (e.g., a user logging in, performing actions, etc.).

You can use testing frameworks such as:

- **Jest**: A JavaScript testing framework that works well with both React (frontend) and Node.js (backend).

- **Mocha** and **Chai**: Testing frameworks for Node.js applications.

- **Cypress**: For end-to-end testing in the browser.

Example of a simple unit test using **Jest**:

javascript

```
// sum.js
function sum(a, b) {
  return a + b;
}

module.exports = sum;
```

javascript

```
// sum.test.js
const sum = require('./sum');

test('adds 1 + 2 to equal 3', () => {
  expect(sum(1, 2)).toBe(3);
});
```

To run the tests:

bash

```
npm test
```

Example: Deploying a Full-Stack App Using Heroku and Netlify

In this example, we will deploy a full-stack application consisting of a **Node.js backend** (Express API) and a **React frontend**. We'll deploy the backend on **Heroku** and the frontend on **Netlify**.

1. Deploying the Backend with Heroku

1. **Set up Heroku**:

    o   If you don't have it, install the Heroku CLI.

    o   Log in to Heroku using the CLI:

    ```bash
    bash


    heroku login
    ```

2. **Prepare the Node.js Backend**:

o Make sure you have a `Procfile` in the root directory of your backend. This tells Heroku how to run your app.

```makefile
web: node server.js
```

o Add a `start` script in your `package.json`:

```json
"scripts": {
  "start": "node server.js"
}
```

3. **Deploy the Backend**:

o Initialize Git in your backend directory if you haven't already:

```bash
git init
```

```
git add .

git commit -m "Initial commit"
```

o   Create a new Heroku app:

```
bash
```

```
heroku create my-backend-app
```

o   Push your code to Heroku:

```
bash
```

```
git push heroku master
```

4. **Open the Heroku App**: After deployment, you can open the app in the browser:

```
bash
```

```
heroku open
```

Your backend should now be running on Heroku.

2. Deploying the Frontend with Netlify

1. **Prepare Your React App**:

   o Build your React app:

   bash

   npm run build

   o The build folder contains the optimized static files that you can deploy to Netlify.

2. **Deploy to Netlify**:

   o Go to the Netlify Dashboard, sign in, and click on **"New Site from Git"**.

   o Connect your GitHub repository, select your repository, and configure the build settings.

     ▪ **Build Command**: npm run build

     ▪ **Publish Directory**: build/

3. **Deploy**:

   o After configuring the settings, Netlify will automatically build and deploy the frontend.

You'll get a URL like `https://your-site-name.netlify.app`.

3. Connect the Frontend and Backend

- In your **React app**, make sure you are sending API requests to the correct URL. For example, if your backend is hosted on Heroku at `https://my-backend-app.herokuapp.com`, update your API calls to use this URL instead of `localhost`.

Example of fetching data from the API:

javascript

```
fetch('https://my-backend-app.herokuapp.com/api/posts')
  .then(response => response.json())
  .then(posts => {
    console.log(posts);
  })
```

```
.catch(error      =>      console.error('Error:',
error));
```

Conclusion

In this chapter, we explored how to deploy a **full-stack JavaScript application** by using **Heroku** for the backend (Node.js) and **Netlify** for the frontend (React). We also discussed the importance of **version control** with Git, organizing your code structure, and writing tests to ensure your application works as expected.

Deployment Best Practices:

1. Use a clear and consistent **folder structure**.

2. Use **version control (Git)** to manage your code and collaborate with others.

3. Automate testing and deployment processes using CI/CD tools.

4. Always **secure sensitive data**, such as environment variables, using services like Heroku's config vars or Netlify's environment variables.

By following these best practices and deployment steps, you can ensure that your application is not only functional but also maintainable and scalable in a production environment.